Praise for Reflections of a Corporate Coach

Richard is a master at showing how coaching models apply in your working day. Spend time with these insights to widen your appreciation of the power of coaching and deepen your skills.

> — Andrew Halfacre, author of
> *First Know What you Want*

I got hooked; *Reflections* is addictive. It is such an easy read, I felt as though you were chatting to me. I could read a small chunk at any time, confident that I would find a little inspiration and thoughtfulness.

The anecdotes are timeless and just as relevant and pertinent to today's climate, sometimes uncannily predicting where we are today.

> — Sarah McDade, Business coach

Reflections of a Corporate Coach
(Volume 1)

Richard Winfield

Editor *CorporateCoach*

Brefi Press

www.brefipress.com

Cover design by Chris Walker, Expressive Design.

First published in 2013 by Brefi Press

ISBN 978-0-948537-03-5

www.brefipress.com

Dedication

John Seymour, Sue Knight and Robert Dilts
who laid the foundations on which I have built

*John Duncan, a 'gentleman' who worked with
me in industry and started his coaching
career as an associate of Brefi Group*

Books by Richard Winfield

Reflections of a Corporate Coach (1-50)

Reflections of a Corporate Coach (51-100)

Stories from a Corporate Coach

Lessons from a Corporate Coach - Coaching

Lessons from a Corporate Coach - Business

www.brefipress.com

About the author

Richard Winfield is the founder and principal consultant of the Brefi Group and head of the Director Development Centre. He is a strategy consultant, facilitator and scenario planner, providing transition coaching to directors, boards and partnerships and helping them develop strategy and build teams.

Richard has a natural talent for collecting, integrating and simplifying ideas and then communicating them to others. He is the guy you call when you need to bring structure and clarity to your thinking. He helps you identify core issues and make the complex simple, holding the space for you to create your own solutions.

Throughout his career he has been committed to community building and getting systems changed to make things better. He is passionate about setting people free to achieve their untapped potential and is continually analysing, simplifying and improving.

A long time student of all forms of executive coaching, Richard has developed both a proprietary course to prepare candidates for professional qualification as executive coaches and the unique Invisible Coaching® process to teach individuals how to think and act like a natural coach.

In the late 1960s Richard gained an honours degree in civil engineering and a master's degree in highways and transportation, followed by a ten-year career as a transportation planner, for which he won an international silver medal. Then in the early 1980s he gained a masters degree in management, followed by careers as a management consultant and publishing entrepreneur, combining interests in business and the impact of public policy.

Since 1990 he has focused on management development and, more recently, on director development and corporate governance.

In 2001 he launched the CorporateCoach newsletter, which has had 20,000 readers.

He launched the Director Development Centre in 2009, combining his interests in strategy and structure with the increasing demand for improved standards of corporate governance.

In 2010 he launched the ASEC School of Executive Coaching to design, license and deliver coach training in Africa, Asia and the Middle East, and in 2011 registered Invisible Coaching® as a proprietary coaching system for individuals.

Richard has extensive consulting experience in the UK, North America, Europe, South and West Africa, Baltic States, Arabian Gulf and South East Asia. He has been involved in business planning roles with companies in America, Europe, the Arabian Gulf and South Africa, including a two and a half year contract for National Power to carry out a full human resource skills analysis, implement a management training programme and introduce an effective management team structure. For three years he was responsible for developing the directors and senior managers of an international engineering group, reporting direct to the chief executive.

Richard is an explorer; he likes exciting new places, exciting new people and exciting new experiences. This is how he has accumulated his knowledge, his wisdom and his rich source of anecdotes.

He is addicted to learning and personal development; he has studied with thought leaders in North America, Europe and Asia, and reads widely.

As well as reading, he enjoys vegetable gardening, landscape gardening and pond building. He has been a farmer, worked as a cowboy and is now an established author.

For further information:

www.richardwinfield.com

Follow me:

www.corporatecoach.co.uk

Twitter.com/rwinfield

Twitter.com/ASECcoach

Twitter.com/directorcoach

Facebook.com/richard.winfield.brefi

Linkedin.com/in/richardwinfield

Foreword

I first met Richard more than two decades ago as the roles of business mentor and sports coach were beginning to merge and tap into the 'Inner Game' approach of Timothy Gallwey and expand on the growing influence of the neuro-linguists John Grinder and Richard Bandler. It was an exciting time intellectually but few people then realised the full potential and impact coaching would have on the business world. Richard was one of those few.

He saw back then how practical and enduring this approach to human excellence would be in an organisational context. He understood that the difference that distinguishes one business from another is not simply the quality of the products, processes and policies, but rather the human factors: the passions, qualities and talents of the unique human beings that bring a business to life.

Since then I have been privileged to watch both up close and at times from afar, as Richard's understanding of human motivation and behaviour has deepened and broadened. Throughout, he has maintained a steady eye on the pragmatic aspects of business and our global economy and has always balanced his approach by aligning his research and development with what is needed in the moment.

His commitment to his own excellence, including

meeting and learning from many of the thought leaders of the day, has been impeccable and I have often been in awe of both the quality and quantity of his achievements. So it was with happy curiosity that I read his *Reflections of a Corporate Coach*. I knew he was a great story teller but I hadn't really had much experience of his writing until now.......and I am delighted to say that he is indeed a fine writer.

These short stories, observations and thoughts are written clearly and simply with a flow and elegance that makes them a pleasure to read. He offers these gems of wisdom and perceptiveness to us as if he is passing a fine bone china plate of delicate pastries around. Bite into any one of these, though, and beneath the well formed structure you will discover plenty of meat. These ideas and perceptions will transform you and your business.

I invite you to be moved, uplifted, paused, challenged and enlightened in the most delicious way. I especially invite you to read Richard's reflections if you are in the midst of a career, leading a business, working in a team or an individual looking for inspiration for your own personal development or next step with any issue or plan.

These pages are bursting with a life's worth of intelligent observation and wit. I have no doubt that there is also much, much more to come and I am already looking forward to it!

Lorraine Calland
Passion@Work Ltd

What is corporate coaching?

Corporate coaching involves coaching in the context of an organisation's vision, mission and values, and towards its goals.

Just as a football coach coaches a football team, a corporate coach coaches an organisation, focusing on the corporate team and corporate vision, mission, values and strategy.

The objective is to raise awareness and clarify goals such that those who have been coached are more able to coach and develop themselves in the future.

This process encourages the development of personal leadership and responsibility throughout the organisation.

Results are measured against the performance requirements of the organisation.

Corporate coaches combine basic coaching skills

with an in-depth understanding of the language, dynamics, processes and culture of organisations – whether these are large companies, SMEs or public sector.

Brefi Group's corporate coaches have MBA level experience and training in the psychology of change. Being qualified in different disciplines broadens and enriches the added value they can bring.

Where does it fit in?

Corporate coaching can take place with individuals or groups. Face-to-face coaching can be supported by telephone or e-mail contact. Corporate coaches can work to a specific schedule or on a retainer, and provide long term support, or be brought in to accelerate change or a specific project.

Where corporate coaching involves coaching a whole organisation in one form or another, it usually requires initial survey work and can overlap into both executive and life coaching. Coaching can arise from a consultancy project or form part of a development programme.

What are the benefits?

Organisations that incorporate coaching into their culture see sustainable improvements in key areas, including internal and external communications, productivity, employee attitudes, and recruitment and retention of staff.

Reflections of a
Corporate Coach
(Volume 1)

Issue No. 1 – February 2001

The Genius is in the simplicity

Last week I went to London to see the musical, The Lion King. It is truly a fantastic and dramatic spectacle. This I had expected, from the reviews that I had heard. What I did not appreciate was how the whole effect was achieved. Counter to the expensive high tech sets of many modern productions, this was ultra low tech. Animals were seen to leap around – but were part of the costume of a dancer, or were mounted on wheels which, when they spun, gave the effect of groups of antelope running. Grass grew and trees swayed – all in the costumes of the actors. Sophisticated but simple.

In West Wales we have a wonderful leisure park – Oakwood. It is a study in the use of gravity. Water slides, toboggan runs, daring drops. Great – great excitement for kids of all ages – but simple.

My son was on an Internet course where they were told about a supermarket chain that ran its e-business by printing out the e-mails, faxing them to the local stores and then sending someone around the shelves with a basket. Great derision from the techies, and how crude an approach!! But that supermarket was the first in the field, has established a lead in the marketplace and has gained practical experience for when it designs its cutting edge automation. Others, developing technical systems first, were left behind in the market. The genius is in the simplicity.

The book review this month is *Built to Last* by Jim Collins and Jerry Porras. I believe that this is THE most important book for leaders in organisations to study. So I was very interested to read about further research being done by Jim Collins. He has been investigating how eleven mediocre companies became great companies. It was not charismatic leaders. He found that the key is a leader who is more like Socrates than Caesar: who led with questions not answers.

For example, Darwin Smith of Kimberly-Clark. For two years he asked simple but powerful questions: "What could Kimberly-Clark be best in the world at?" "What would ignite its passions?" "What would best drive its economic engine?" Quietly but insistently, sparking internal argument, he searched for a penetrating understanding of the organisation's future. Then he settled on a radical change and 25 years later Kimberly-Clark was beating Proctor & Gamble in six out of eight paper product categories.

The genius is in the simplicity – just asking questions. A coaching approach.

Issue No. 2 – April 2001

An unintended disaster

This morning the cows across the valley were let out for the first time this year, streaming across the field, enjoying the fresh grass and their freedom. Yesterday evening, having just finished reading our book of the month, I took a walk down to the bridge; sheep quietly grazing and a total of four pairs of geese flying home up the river.

The British countryside is a joy to experience.

A few weeks ago I wondered why several huge earth movers on Brecon bypass were being escorted by police, and why I then came upon more than thirty police standing on the roadside. I have since driven several times past Eppynt, where signs along the roadside proclaim 'The Valley of Death', and driven along the Wye Valley near Hay, where huge fires raged in the distance.

There can be few industries where loss of stock can have such a deep emotional impact as in farming – or where it can threaten the loss of tourist environments generated over hundreds of years.

I don't suppose that when politicians and civil servants in Europe and Westminster introduced regulations to control abattoirs or when they decided to make annual premium payments for sheep (which resulted in transporting animals on long journeys), they intended to create a disaster situation out of a potential local outbreak of foot-and-mouth disease.

We live in a system. Everything we do, whether in our travel, in our work or in our communications, takes

3

place in systems. And increasingly these systems can be global. Systems react to change. And if we consider only the direct impact of our actions, we can later be taken by surprise by the unintended consequences. However, if we study the systems, perhaps we can anticipate the cumulative effect. Understanding of systems dynamics is one of the competencies required by the International Coach Federation for executive coaches.

What we do affects what our customers do. It also affects what our competitors do – and this can affect what the market does. Classic consideration: what is the likely impact of a price cut – winning customers, starting a lose-lose price war or expanding the total market?

I am becoming increasingly involved with clients' Internet strategies. On the face of it the Internet is wonderful news. Better communications lead to procurement savings, access to larger markets and faster development of new products. The Internet will bring major benefits to mankind by speeding and spreading learning. On the face of it we can expect more growth and better profits. But beware. Better communication and transparency means more competition and continuous pressure on prices – and lower profits. Consumers will benefit, but the major companies whose shares provide for our pensions may suffer much lower returns in the future. An unexpected consequence?

Earlier this month I managed to attend a performance of the play 'Copenhagen', by Michael Frayn. In 1941 the German physicist Werner Heisenberg made a strange trip to Copenhagen to see his Danish counterpart, Niels Bohr. They were old friends, and their work together had opened the way into the atom. But now they were on opposite sides of a world war. During the meeting they went out for a walk and returned unexpectedly soon, after 15 minutes. Nobody knows what happened between them.

The play takes place in the afterlife, when they and Bohr's wife meet again to discuss their memories of what happened, and what it led to.

During the rest of the war, Heisenberg led the failed German effort to achieve nuclear fission. After the war he was snubbed and rejected by other nuclear scientists. Bohr went to America to join the team that developed the atom bomb, and was celebrated.

The play runs through three interpretations of what might have happened. Gradually as possibilities are explored, it becomes clear that perhaps Heisenberg should have been celebrated because he was very successful at failing to develop a bomb for Germany. Did he or did he not understand the mathematics. And did Bohr or did he not explain the implication of the mathematics. Had Heisenberg not managed to maintain his lead in Germany he would have been replaced by a Nazi competitor who, quite possibly, might have succeeded with a bomb. So, intentionally or unintentionally, Heisenberg saved Europe from the atom bomb!

A dramatic demonstration of how things can be understood from different perspectives. Such a skill is essential in successful negotiations.

Editor's note: You can find an article on perceptual positions on the Brefi Group web site.

Issue No. 3 – May 2001

Words matter

Who is the most important person in your organisation?

I spend a lot of time travelling to and from London on Chiltern Trains. This company is one of the smallest of the train operating companies and is reckoned to be the best. Certainly, my experience has been excellent.

In the 1980s, bus companies discovered that one of the benefits of replacing large buses with minibuses was that instead of attempting to teach bus drivers customer care, they were able to recruit shop assistants and others who understood customer care – and teach them to drive. Much better passenger relations was the result. Chiltern Trains has been able to take a similar approach. Also, they have given the staff very smart uniforms and fully involved them in the running of the railway – such that they are known as Adrian's family, because of their close relationship with managing director Adrian Shooter.

To answer my question, the most important person on Chiltern Trains is the steward who pushes the buffet trolley. Mostly young, these are bright, friendly people who manage the passenger environment and are able to dispense free drinks if anything should go wrong.

There is one habit that Chiltern has picked up that I wonder whether they have thought through – that of referring to everyone as 'customers". Maybe we are customers when we buy our tickets. But when on the train, surely we are passengers. I recognise that they are trying to instil the concept of 'customer' care in the staff, but I doubt whether any hotel, for example, would choose to destroy the concept of 'host' by downgrading its 'guests' into 'customers'.

In our work as corporate coaches, we listen carefully to words and language; they reveal a lot about the values and metaphors of an organisation. A slight change of language can lead to major changes in behaviour. Disney, for example, puts great emphasis on using 'guest' and 'cast member' for visitor and staff.

Issue No. 4 – July 2001

A lesson in the fingers

My fingers sometimes compete to see which hand can reach the key first – with unfortunate results in my spelling. I was checking the website recently when I spotted a common transposition in the word 'from'. The title to the page read: "Learning Resources form Brefi Group". I was about to change it when it occurred to me that it was a very good description of what we are about. We are a learning organisation, and we are influenced by the learning resources we discover.

Our reviews this month feature Tim Gallwey's Inner Game. He believes strongly in a balance between the rewards that come from performance, the enjoyment that comes from the experience and the learning or growth that takes place. He says: "When performance alone is the goal, and learning and enjoyment are neglected, it isn't long before performance itself evens off or sometimes declines." I have met several organisations recently that are very target and performance driven – and where senior staff are concerned about imminent collapse through burn-out. Coaching is a way for individuals to get their work into balance and maintain energy and enthusiasm.

An example of where enthusiasm can revive an organisation is MG Rover. For much of my life the Austin Longbridge plant, which is now the home of MG Rover, was held up as a symbol of all that was worst in British industry. BMW failed to turn it round and wrote it off as 'The English Patient'. Then last year, in the face of threatened closure, a small under-funded consortium led by

8

John Towers took it over. I was privileged last week to have a tour of the plant and talk with Towers. What a lot they have achieved in only nine months!

This week they launch a new range of MG vehicles, widely praised by the motoring press. Their next challenge is to replace the Rover 45 model. General opinion is that there is no way that they can fund a new model. But Towers disagrees. He believes there are real advantages in being a small company. He claims that the MG developments could not have been achieved by a traditional company, with their committees, marketing departments and focus groups. He told his team: "You know what MGs should be. Now go away and create them. There will be no formal presentations, but we will keep in contact and my door is always open." And . . "If anyone is found near a focus group they will be sacked!"

MG Rover is part owned by its staff and by its dealers. Towers believes that he has already proved that if engineers and designers are allowed to get on with their jobs, use their own judgement and work in partnership with suppliers, then great cars can be developed at low cost.

Here is an organisation that is learning as well as performing – and clearly enjoying the experience. And I noticed that the new cars carry a Union Jack.

Issue No. 5 – August 2001

Who should we be coaching?

Who should we be coaching and what's in it for us?

With budget under scrutiny it is easy to understand why the questions on the mind of many prospective clients are:

- Who should we be coaching?
- What will it deliver for my business?

A survey of senior executives of twenty-five blue chip organisations, designed to assess the effectiveness of coaching as a management development tool was recently quoted in the *Journal of Management Development*. It revealed an across-the-board consensus of UK senior executives that coaching was one of the most powerful strategic and tactical weapons open to businesses today because of its ability to enhance areas of executive expertise that were already at a high level and to establish skills that were previously absent or weak.

The same survey quoted a respondent who recommended that UK executives learn from the US. "...where people are actually often proud to admit that they are being coached because they see it as indicating the importance their employer attaches to them. In the US it is taken for granted that performance will improve significantly as a result of coaching, although certainly it is also accepted that deep-rooted negative attitudes and behaviours will take time – perhaps several months – to shift."

There are abundant courses on which to learn technical skills and conferences to keep up to date in this fast moving industry. However, the kind of learning which puts all this expertise to best use is an unconscious process.

Those managers who coach can give important feedback and training. A specialist coach provides a structured, outcomes led process to create outstanding performance – both improving the performance of the executive and demonstrating a process he/she can use with their team.

We can learn a lot about coaching from parents 'teaching' children to ride a bike. We support them when they start, we encourage, we reduce risks where we can, but we do not teach the highly intricate balance required while pushing alternate pedals. The process rapidly becomes an unconscious skill and this is when we are at our most effective.

Can we still learn like this as adults? Well, yes. Most of us learned to drive a car and now do so with little thought about much of the process, our awareness, importantly, being directed at what is around us.

I experienced a direct example of the speed of unconscious learning over the weekend, when I injured my right hand to the point that I couldn't even lift a kettle without excruciating pain. Initially, I found my conscious mind telling me to use the other hand. Rapidly, however, my left hand became dominant for all activities – no thought required!

When one applies this analogy in the business setting it is easy to see the value that can be added to individual and team performance when conscious 'tools' can become subconsciously understood and used. How often do we see people 'working hard' after a training course to apply their learning? In the early days they may struggle consciously to change old habits, but so often they eventually return to their old behaviour.

Coaching will enable them to retain and apply the learning. Enhancement of the learning process through coaching makes this easy and delivers greater results for less effort. Coaching can help the unconscious deliver what is hard work for the conscious mind!

The expert executive coach will combine specialist skills in communication at conscious and unconscious levels to help clients identify direction and overcome obstacles on their path to success.

So who should we be coaching?

Coaching performs at all levels of an organisation, particularly in high performers and at the top where there are less role models and precedents, and maximum leverage can be achieved.

What is in it for the business?

Consider an executive earning £50,000; overheads increase this by two and a half times and the company makes a net profit of 10%. This means that at the margin the company needs a turnover of £1.25 million to cover his/her costs! An expensive asset to release for training courses, and certainly an asset that must perform at its maximum potential!

Coaching helps set better goals, and reach goals faster, make better decisions and improve relationships. An effective process for achieving business results and gaining more for less.

It requires limited time, is work related and outcome oriented to make an executive more effective – or to remove blockages that frustrate performance. Minimum time input and maximum performance improvement.

The higher the pay, the more appropriate executive coaching becomes. Coaching at the top has the greatest leverage on corporate performance.

Issue No. 6 – September 2001

Time for a PEST

President Kennedy and UK Prime Minister Harold Macmillan struck up a personal friendship. When the young Jack asked his elderly mentor what he feared most, he is reported to have been told: "Events, dear boy, events."

We have had plenty of events during this month and many leaders in business as well as politics will have had cause to consider the significance of his reply.

It is widely reported in the media that the world has changed. Perhaps, more accurately, our perception of the world has changed, and it is our response that has caused the economy to change. From the initial response of anger, we have moved to questioning what we have done to cause these events.

Another question might be: "What could be the results caused by what we are now doing, or considering doing?" As all organisations are faced with a changed environment, so it is time for some scenario planning.

For many companies, the next three months are the season for strategy; planning in preparation of the budget for the next financial year. They may well include a SWOT (Strengths, Weaknesses, Opportunities and Threats) and PEST (Political, Economic, Sociological, Technological) analyses. This year it will be particularly important to include a PEST analysis.

What are some of the processes that we coach individuals, organisations and governments that might be particularly relevant just now?

- Firstly, the ability to second position – to review a

situation from another's perspective, and to do so in some depth, experiencing their emotions and seeing one's self from their position.

- Secondly, the ability to third position – to take a detached view in an unemotional state.
- Thirdly, recognition that the world as we see it might not be the same as the world as others see it.
- Fourthly, recognition that the meaning of a communication is the response it elicits – not what we meant to say, but the impact on and the response of the recipient, who may or may not have been the intended target.

Issue No. 7 – October 2001

Discovering differences

If there is a good thing that has come out of the terrorist attacks on America it is recognition of how little the West and the Muslim world know about each other.

Building rapport requires an understanding of the other party's perception – what we would call their map of the world – and Western governments and individuals are rapidly recognising the depth of their ignorance about Islam and the spread of fundamentalism.

In my early days in the USA, I had great difficulty following directions. Americans think in terms of travelling along roads ("follow Archibald and then take Vineyard, north") – in Britain we think in terms of travelling between junctions and landmarks ("turn left at the Nag's Head"). Two ways of communicating the same message – but completely different mental maps.

I have been working on a business plan to establish a company in France. And the same applies. The French use codified law – laws and regulations are written down to give permission. In Britain, case law is flexible, evolves with use and prohibits behaviour. Tax is different too. Nothing is complicated – but to a stranger it seems, well, strange!

I have worked in the public and private sectors and in government, and different mental models apply in each.

How often do we waste time and cause confusion because we have not taken the trouble to discover the other party's model of the world? After all, if the meaning of the communication is the response it elicits, then if we cannot anticipate the response, we cannot expect to communicate effectively.

360 degree feedback enables us to discover how other people perceive us, as well as how well we are performing.

Issue No. 8 – November 2001

Doing away with the tolerations

It is Sunday, and I am at home. This afternoon I took a walk down to Gogoyan Bridge to lean on the parapet and watch the Teifi flow determinedly towards the sea. There were two swans below the bridge. Grazing above the bridge were two more swans and three fully grown cygnets. Some ducks flew up the valley. There was birdsong.

The hillside opposite was beautiful in the soft autumn light, with the rich green of the fields and the brown of the bracken. People were paragliding in the thermals rising from the west facing slope.

Last Sunday I was in Birmingham for the CBI exhibition. The previous weekend I had been home to pick the last of my runner beans, but very often I am away two weekends in three. Why do I spend so much time away from home?

In life coaching there is a concept known as 'tolerations'. Things that you put up with, which sap your energy and which you would endeavour to leave out if you designed your life from scratch. Very often, things that you take for granted – that have developed gradually.

Executives are under a lot of pressure and need support to overcome very basic fears (though they are not so eager to acknowledge it as fear).

Husbands and wives have 'tolerated' the stress for the sake of the company – and it has damaged both family and company.

On a larger scale, we have tolerated terrorism as long as it has been kept on a limited scale and, preferably, happens elsewhere.

But, now, we have discovered the true cost of living with terrorism. No longer are we prepared to tolerate the situation, and already there is sign of faster progress towards resolution of conflicts in Northern Ireland and the Middle East.

So the question for all of us, as individuals, organisations and nations, is what do we tolerate that we would not put up with if we took the trouble to review the situation?

And what's the cost of continuing to put up with such things? Divorce? A heart attack? Company failure?

Whatever you are doing, you probably deserve better. So, stop putting up with things that impoverish your life.

Issue No. 9 – December 2001

Developing more powerful business leaders

The end of 2001 has been a busy time for the UK team at Brefi Group. We have been building a business base in Birmingham, culminating in a privately hosted breakfast event at one of the main theatres in the city.

Some thirty guests had an excellent discussion and we thought you might like to know of some of the themes that emerged:

Communication – Peter Wall of lawyers Wragge & Co introduced this subject with comments about the value not only of talking to your staff but of taking an interest in them, asking them what they thought were the problems and managing their expectations.

Promotion of fee earners – this was a key concern of accountants and lawyers present. Their firms depend on the effectiveness of their top fee earners. But they also depend on the strategy and management of the firm. How should you select your managers? And, what training do they need as they move into a management role?

Development of senior staff – several speakers from the floor explained their company's process for training junior staff, but commented that they had no equivalent for senior staff. Once promoted, they had to sink or swim.

Personality traits – there was some discussion about whether you can train people, or whether their behaviour depends on their personality.

Qualifications – John Phillips of the Institute of

Directors gave statistics about how few managers and directors had professional qualifications, and Chris Monk explained how Birmingham Forward is focusing on skills and education for people working in knowledge based businesses as part of its campaign to attract companies to Birmingham.

Role modelling – Many people at the top fail to recognise the impact of their own behaviour on others. An example given was of people who prefer to work at home, ignoring the impact of their absence in the workplace and the message it sends.

At Brefi Group we have set our sights specifically on helping develop senior managers and directors so that they and their organisations can fulfil their potential. Guests at our breakfast event confirmed our own experience that even in organisations that invest in training and development there is a tendency to ignore the people at the top.

But, who has the greatest impact on the organisation?

The end of year is a time for looking back and reviewing progress. How effectively did you set objectives at this time last year? How effective were you in achieving them? What impact did they have? We include for your revision at this season some notes on setting well-formed outcomes.

Perhaps one objective for the coming year should be to recognise that lifelong learning is for everyone – including yourself.

In a recent interview, the managing partner of a law practice told me: "We all agree that everyone else must change!" So, whoever, you are – at the top of an organisation, or in a more junior position – we challenge you to recognise your potential, and make appropriate resolutions.

I have included a poem by Marianne Williamson that

was used by Nelson Mandela in his inaugural speech.

In 2002, let your own light shine, and thereby give other people permission to do the same.

Our Deepest Fear

"Our deepest fear
is not that we are inadequate.
Our deepest fear is that we are
powerful beyond measure.
It is our light, not our darkness,
that most frightens us.
We ask ourselves,
who am I to be brilliant,
successful, talented and fabulous?
Actually, who are you NOT to be?
You are a child of God.
Your playing small doesn't serve the world.
There's nothing enlightened about shrinking
so that other people
won't feel insecure around you.
We were born to make manifest
the glory that is within us.
It's not just in some of us;
it's in EVERYONE!
And as we let our own light shine,
we unconsciously give other people
permission to do the same.
As we are liberated from our own fear,
our presence automatically liberates others!"

Issue No. 10 – January 2002

Education – the foundation of progress

We have passed the stage where a nation's economy is dependent on its raw materials. Oil, agriculture and minerals – even location – are increasingly irrelevant.

Today the most important resource is the talent of the population, and we can assume that all populations have similar potential.

The difference is in the creativity and the competence of the people – a function of culture and education, but primarily education. That apart, success depends on infrastructure – transport, communications, law, banking etc.

It is a tragedy to watch countries either imploding or destroying themselves when they deny rights to educated people, persecute entrepreneurs or physically destroy the infrastructure – often because of prejudice against a different tribe, race, religion or culture, or because corruption takes over from law.

What can companies do to avoid such self-destruction and to encourage development of their people?

The metaphor of the Russian dolls is that managers have the choice between recruiting people who are 'bigger' than them – or who are 'smaller'. Done successively, the outcome is obvious. Of my clients some of the most notable have been those who have taken real delight in following the successful careers of ex-employees whom they have recruited and developed and who have since gone on to far greater things.

And then there are others who say: "If we develop these people, some of them will leave." Perhaps they will.

But, if they have any initiative and you don't give them an opportunity to grow they will probably leave anyway!

Rather, develop them and enjoy the benefit while they are with you. They will attract other bright people and encourage others to make the effort to develop themselves. The result is a general uplift of the aspiration and performance of the organisation.

Companies like Ford of Europe recognised this and set a lead by subsidising any form of training and development for their staff – regardless of its relevance to the individual's job. They believe that all personal development is worthwhile and that if employees start to enjoy learning they will also start to learn on the job.

Perhaps part of the personal development programme could involve making a contribution to local schools or young entrepreneurs, where a partnership will bring benefits to both sides.

In a learning organisation groups can learn together. Brefi Group specialises in working with senior people to set a lead in self-development for business benefits and in introducing a learning culture throughout the organisation.

Issue No. 11 – February 2002

Self-confidence – or self-esteem?

A fundamental part of our business in both executive coaching and organisation development is that our work helps individuals, teams and organisations develop self-esteem. We believe that if we achieve this, then they will operate more effectively; there will be greater trust, more empowerment and greater creativity. We also believe that people – and their families – will be able to live more fulfilling lives.

So it was very worrying to read in the British press recently about research that appeared to suggest that, contrary to what had traditionally been believed, high self-esteem led to bullying and crime.

Not at all in line with our aspirations.

However, further analysis revealed that there had been confusion in the reporting between self-confidence and self-esteem. Self-esteem leads to self-confidence. But self-confidence need not lead to self-esteem.

Self-esteem is respect for self. It gives the confidence to decide to do what is right even when others are foolish or criminal because "I am better than that". It is very important for teenagers when they are under peer pressure to smoke, shop lift or take drugs. It is also important in business, where the equivalent could be fraud or crime.

One of our missions is to promote leadership and to help raise groups out of cynicism. One cry we hear is about the fashion for 'partnership'. The belief is often that partnership means that "we give and they take". In an extreme, the cry of a supplier: "If we don't screw them first, they'll screw us." What behaviour is such belief likely to lead to? Just the sort of behaviour that will, indeed, elicit a negative response from the customer or client – and a deteriorating relationship.

Another belief we hold is that the meaning of the communication is the response it elicits. In other words, we are responsible for the consequences.

If another party reacts badly, what responsibility should we take, and in such circumstances how could we behave differently to achieve the outcome we desire. And in systems terms, how does our behaviour this time affect their behaviour next time?

It applies in business. It applies in teams. And it applies in social relationships and within families. How we behave affects how others behave; thus, the difference between leadership and followership.

You may be surprised by the title of the book that we review in this issue of the newsletter. Hardly the title you would expect for a business audience. But Flirt Coach is about communication for success. If communication is a generic skill, why not learn it in a fun context. And I have an excuse, of course. February includes St Valentine's Day.

But to return to self-confidence and self-esteem. How did the confusion arise? In a reaction against too much criticism of children, parents were encouraged to focus on praising instead. Good advice, but only when their actions deserve it. In the words of The One Minute Manager, "Catch someone doing something good".

Or, as one of the press articles said: "If you give the child feedback on what they have done, then the child can praise itself." That leads to self-esteem and self-confidence – and the same applies in business. Quality feedback improves morale and allows people to improve their performance.

Praise or criticism unrelated to the act causes confusion. So the objective is not to make people feel good, but to enable them to feel good "because . . ."

Issue No. 12 – March 2002

Significant Decisions

In the early 1970s I worked on a project for London Transport to track the position of buses on London's Route 11. This was a long route crossing London from Liverpool Street to Hammersmith and was notorious for traffic delays causing buses to arrive in bunches – a banana route. "None come and then three come at once!"

I am sorry to say that *CorporateCoach* is getting a bit like that. The March issue is running into April and then, hopefully, the April issue will follow rapidly behind.

Before I worked for London Transport I was a driver of one of 20 coaches carrying 500 students by land between Britain and India – a thirteen-week round trip of cultural events. We stopped overnight on the way out at a campsite in Istanbul, where one of the definitive moments in my life took place.

We were sitting around a fire singing and chatting to Colonel Gregory, who was the organiser of this Commonwealth Expedition. Someone passed him a paper bag of mixed sweets. He put in his hand, took out a sweet and put it into his mouth. I was amazed.

For me, choosing a sweet was a decision. It required attention, and some thought; maybe only for a moment, but it required a decision. How could Greg just put in his hand with no attention to what he chose?

Well, of course, the choice of sweet was insignificant to him and justified no thought whatsoever.

I wonder how much time and attention is given to decisions, whose outcome is insignificant. Indeed, how much attention is given to events that have happened and cannot now be affected?

And, when there is a shortage of time, how much time is given to less significant decisions at the expense of much more important matters? Examine a typical meeting, board meeting or committee meeting and I am sure you will find some examples.

I came across a recent example in a company that moved to new premises and needed a telephone system. Much time was devoted to obtaining quotations and analysing the differences. Clearly, good value is important. But the difference between the systems offered was insignificant. The delay in making a choice was significant – staff could not operate effectively and sales were lost.

If you wish to be effective, differentiate between decisions of different significance and concentrate on those that matter.

Issue No. 13 – April 2002

Our attitudes affect our staff development

I have been reading Brian Keenan's account of his time as a hostage in Beirut and his relationship with his kidnappers. One of them wanted Brian to give him English lessons. A passage he found in a textbook was based on the well-worn cliché that "'one man's terrorist is another man's freedom fighter". Keenan says that his student's reading was good but he was convinced that the reader had little knowledge of the meaning, and so tried to explain what it was about.

"I quickly became aware of something that I was to become convinced of during my time with these men – that their capacity for conceptual thoughts was severely underdeveloped. To try to teach any language, which is overwhelmingly about meaning, to someone who does not have any kind of analytical capacity is extremely wearying."

I read recently in the press that in the UK a large percentage of children starting school in inner city areas are underdeveloped in their learning and social skills. They have not had the conversation and interaction; they have not been read to and challenged, and they have not had creative play opportunities that are expected in a healthy upbringing. As a result, they are set some 18 months behind the norm for their age.

As managers we can influence and stretch our staff by the stimulation we give to them at work and our attitude to their abilities. As Sue Knight says in the second edition of *NLP at Work*, "We influence others by the beliefs we hold in them, irrespective of the facts or the circumstances. If I can see the confident part in you, my interactions with you invite that part of you to emerge."

Issue No. 14 – June 2002

The value of reflection

I had to get up early recently to take part in an interview on Radio 5 Live on time management. The theme of the programme was: "What would you do with an extra hour each day?"

I answered, "I would *do* nothing. I would use it for quiet reflection."

I have been publishing the new newsletter *Career Coach*, edited by Margaret Stead. In the May editorial she describes a phone call to her mother in hospital. Her mother said she was enjoying her stay because it was giving her more time to 'reflect'.

Margaret says that in years of interviewing senior people and asking them to look back, they say that if they could lead their lives again they would be more 'reflective'. They got so caught up in the doing that they often lost sight of the meaning.

What would you do with an extra hour? Would you use it to achieve more – or to improve the quality of your life? Is there a difference? Your choice – your life.

Executive coaching is getting an increasingly high profile. It is interesting to report what others say. Here is an extract from the *Sunday Telegraph* Business File:

Coaching can be useful when:

- you are newly promoted to the board
- learning to chair meetings
- addressing staff
- making board decisions
- directing change

- dealing with tension at home
- handling tricky staff
- managing stress

Issue No. 15 – October 2002

Growth of executive coaching

Talking to people in the business world, there still appears to be a lot of uncertainty out there and many organisations are reining in their budgets. What is interesting though is that the use of executive coaching continues to grow even in these challenging times.

Coaching is surviving (and growing) because it is actually delivering results both for the organisation and for the individual. People being coached are seeing that they are becoming more effective and delivering better results for their business.

And that is the key. The coaching must be focused on the business context and delivering a real impact to the bottom line. Coaching that doesn't do this can be a pleasant and positive experience for the individual and yet the organisation doesn't benefit as much as it might.

When times are tough, people feel increased pressure to deliver and, perhaps, to hold on to their jobs. At times like this, it is only through a solution tailored to the specific needs of the business that results can be achieved quickly – general interventions take too long to work, if ever.

Time pressure is intense and coaching can achieve significant benefits for as little as two hours a month; allowing the executive to stand back and gain a new perspective on their situation leading to better focused decisions and actions.

So, despite the challenging, fast-moving and uncertain times that we live in, and maybe even because of these things, excellent Executive Coaching is delivering real business benefit when targeted at senior executives and managers – the people who can make the biggest difference.

Issue No. 16 – November 2002

Lessons from an 'Afronaut'

Mark Shuttleworth is the first African to go into space, the second space tourist and an Internet billionaire. He is 28 years old.

He recently gave a presentation to the South African Business Club in London. The theme of his talk was that his life had just been a series of fortunate coincidences. He claimed, for instance, that he only studied business because he noticed on his first days at university that there were lots of girls on that course.

But the tone of his presentation was one of great enthusiasm for everything that he does. He repeatedly used words like 'passion' and 'fascinated'. Since his success in business and his trip into space he has committed a great deal of time and energy in South Africa to visiting schools and supporting entrepreneurs in order to give them a role model of success from an environment that they can relate to.

So, what were the lessons he has learned? Well, two things from his time in space – how thin is the ozone layer, and what the earth looks like without seeing national boundaries. He says that in future everyone should have the opportunity to go into space just to experience these two things.

From a business and personal perspective, several things stood out. First, doing what you really want to do. "I find that often there are things we would really love to do, that we actually can do – so why don't we?" In his case, he realised that his wish to go into space was a reachable dream, so he did it.

Second, he found that it was useful being in South Africa and *not* being in Silicon Valley. It enabled him to stand away from the crowd. "It is important to run with the herd, but it is also important to get ahead of it. Of course this didn't necessarily make sense to those around me at the time. All my role models have that in common: that they are willing to be thought of as complete nuts."

He stressed the need to read widely, and to differentiate between the news – the noise – and the prevailing wisdom. "Newspapers look at the edge of the bell curve – look at the mass of the curve." It is important to be able to question the prevailing wisdom.

Mark was very impressed with the training provided by the Russians. He spent seven months with them. He concluded that a lot of the training was more to do with pushing the envelope of confidence and experience than specifically the training and the skills involved. He discovered that fear is in the anticipation, not the actual. When he walked out to the rocket he was calm – he was ready for it.

Perhaps our theme should be: "Find the passion and you will find the potential."

Issue No. 17 – January 2003

Seize the day – or wait

The start of a new year is traditionally a time for reviewing progress and making resolutions. And late January is the time when many people realise that they have already forgotten about their well meant decisions to change!

A worthy new year resolution would be to take better decisions. In fact, this will not get you very far. Your coach would ask you to re-word this to "apply better decision making processes in order to take better decisions". Our coaching tip in this issue will help you here.

Sometimes a first stage of making a decision is to decide whether to make a decision at all and when to do so. We live in a fast moving world and opportunities and decisions are thrown at us all the time. It is easy to get caught up in the need to respond at the same rate.

Many years ago I moved into a new area and had a large pond dug. The contractor came round with the invoice and wanted to be paid. I was a little concerned but wanted to make a good impression as a new resident. Overnight, I realised that the work had not been completed to my specification and I had been charged for the contractor's own problems. Since then, it has been a principle never to pay an invoice without 24 hours to consider it.

There are situations that are self healing. If you do nothing they will go away. However, there are other situations that fester. The longer you leave a decision, the worse the situation becomes.

There are also cases where there is a window of opportunity. An unwillingness to commit or a desire to negotiate just that little bit more can lose the whole deal.

Untangling the reality of a situation is an area where a coach can provide real value. After all; there is no point in having a good process for making the wrong sort of decision.

Issue No. 18 – March 2003

Scenarios for better boards

This issue covers two of my favourite subjects; scenario planning and the effectiveness of boards of directors. I believe they are subjects where we can add particular value as coach/facilitators, as well as areas in which commercial organisations can improve their own effectiveness.

There is to be a major improvement in the UK of how boards of directors are appointed and developed. This will be a big challenge to many companies. Although the Higgs Review focuses on the appointment of non-executive directors, it also covers development of directors and performance evaluation of whole boards. A key role of non-executive directors is to constructively challenge proposals from the executive. This requires communication skills similar to that of a coach and demands a change of style and mindset for most directors, who tend to come from an executive background.

The new requirements look set to open directorships to a wider range of candidate and to foster a greater application of good practice for appointment, appraisal and development of individuals and teams at the highest level.

One of the biggest challenges to scenario planners is not so much being creative as letting go of established assumptions. Recent world events have made this much easier. We have had ten years to accept the end of the Cold War and to observe the dramatic changes that have ensued.

More recently, we have seen events that will help us

unfreeze other stable assumptions: the Internet, environmental change, AIDS, mass migration, global terrorism, changing international alliances. Whether you welcome these or not, they have reminded us that fundamental assumptions may not hold forever. These changes may have increasing impact over ten years (or 30 years), and over a period of ten years we can expect more changes that we can't forecast.

In these circumstances we are likely to be more open to scenario thinking – and certainly more aware of the need to carry out scenario planning.

I am delighted to discover that *The Mind of a Fox* is now available from Amazon. Last year I attended a lecture by Clem Sunter based on a book that had been circulating within the South African business community. At that time the book was not available in the UK so I arranged to import half a dozen copies. I lobbied the publishers to make it available on Amazon so that I could promote it more widely. And at last it is here.

I am in the process of moving house and have had to clear out both an attic and a large barn. In one case we are selling an antique. When discussing the deal with the auctioneer I was struck when, instead of the negative "No problem" response that is so common, he said: "We'll do our best for you." I liked that.

I also found an old personal organiser of my son's. The first page was a mission statement: "To recognise my potential and go for it." It could be a universal theme!

Issue No. 19 – July 2003

Keep it simple

This is the first of four issues in July. In this issue and the next we bring you up to date with some of our activities and products. Future issues will include articles by two of my colleagues who work in the recruitment business. As coaches we believe that everybody has the capacity to perform better, and that our processes will help them achieve more of their potential. However, there is such a thing as a square peg in a round hole. It is in nobody's interest to try to improve somebody in the wrong situation. The Disney organisation believes very strongly in recruiting by values – and that it is then their responsibility to find where an individual can make the best contribution. When this does not work, they say: "We have a values conflict here," and agree to part company.

Much better to put effort into recruiting.

I have recently returned from a very successful scenario planning project in the USA. The interesting thing was that, in a very high tech environment, scenario planning identified the biggest issue as a simple 'human' one. Not what the participants were expecting, but the revelation was welcomed by all.

The other surprise was their amazement at my use of 'Blu-tack' for holding up flip chart sheets. Apparently, this soft blue malleable material is unknown in Washington. It and a few felt tip pens are the basis of my travel anywhere pack. Much more powerful than PowerPoint!

One of my favourite stories appeared in the *Readers' Digest* many years ago. A grandmother was reading a picture book with her grandson, who lived on a farm.

> First picture: "What's that?"
> "It's a lion."
> "Very good."
> Second picture: "What's that?"
> "It's a zebra."
> "That's right, very good."
> Third picture: "What's that?"
> "An elephant."
> "Very good."
> Fourth picture: "And here's an easy one, what's that?"
> "I don't know."
> "Come on, you know this one."
> "No, I am not sure."
> "Come on now."
> "I think it might be a Charolais cross Simmental!!!!"

The meaning of the question is a function of the context. What was a cow to the grandmother was something far more sophisticated to the little boy.

I got caught out on this recently. I am interested in the techniques used for sales, and am often surprised by the methods used by many established sales forces. Had it not been for major thunderstorms grounding my plane at another airport, I would have flown down to Texas during my recent trip to the USA to meet Sharon Drew Morgen and discuss her new book. Her 'Buying Facilitation®' takes a coaching approach to helping the buyer buy, rather than the seller sell. But this is a huge cultural change for traditional sales people.

In a recent presentation I was asked about our expertise in sales. I tried to determine whether they wanted a Charolais or a Simmental – when all they wanted was a cow!! Sometimes a cigar is just a cigar!

The old saying, "Keep it simple, stupid" still applies.

Issue No. 20 – July 2003

Leading with BHAGs

I have been reading two books by Christopher Reeve (*Still Me* and *Nothing is Impossible*).

I had heard of Christopher Reeve as "some actor with a broken neck who foolishly thinks he will be able to walk". The books contradict this view. Reeve is a determined actor with a strong desire to learn. After a serious fall from his horse he broke his neck and became a paraplegic. For most people, this would have been the end of an active life. After three months their medical insurance would end and they would live out a subsistence existence. Reeve is different. His commitment to learning, his high profile and access to the highest in the land, and his fortunate wealth, have enabled him to do what others could not.

When he issued his personal challenge it was not just to keep himself positive. It was the same as President Kennedy committing the USA to getting a man on the moon and back safely before the end of the decade.

"In my conversations with scientists working on repairing the damaged spinal cord, I've often repeated my desire to stand on my fiftieth birthday and drink a toast to everyone who has helped me. Whether or not this will actually happen is not really the point. My purpose has been to start a ticking clock that might help motivate everyone working in the field. This strategy seems to have had a powerful effect. A leading investigator stated that up until a few years ago there was some sort of breakthrough about once a year but that important new discoveries are now being made around twice a month." In fact, Reeve has passed his deadline without being able to stand. However, he has made enormous progress himself in ways that were previously believed to be impossible and has regained significant muscle control.

More significantly, he has challenged and changed the laws and budgets of his country and stimulated research. There is a real possibility that he will achieve his personal aim.

In their book *Built to Last,* Collins and Porras suggest that the first method of preserving the core and stimulating progress that distinguishes visionary companies from the comparison companies is the setting of Big Hairy Audacious Goals (BHAGs) – commitment to challenging, audacious goals and projects toward which a visionary company channels its efforts.

Christopher Reeve's books are a joy for anyone interested in personal development. They also generate great respect for someone who not only survived against all odds, but commits himself to several hours a day of hard exercise and is prepared to take risks to travel and promote his cause.

One aspect of leadership is the ability to stimulate, stretch and motive a team. Another is to be prepared to support it by example. "What BHAG would make the most difference in your business or personal life?"

Issue No. 21 – July 2003

Sharon Drew Morgen

I have been interested to note the reaction of colleagues when I have told them about Sharon Drew Morgen's visit this week. Those who have read her books are very excited. Those who have not, just have a blank look. It appears that she is known in the UK mainly through her books.

I thought you might be interested to learn a little more about her. It would be so disappointing if you realised, after the event, what you had missed!

Sharon Drew Morgen is an international entrepreneur, business consultant, sales trainer, author, keynote speaker, and general paradigm buster. In each role, she draws on the experience of being a life-long student of communications, as well as a multi-million dollar sales producer who created her own unique business environment and brand selling.

Her success comes from putting people first. Concepts like trust, integrity, values, relationship, rapport, respect, and win-win collaboration have long been central to her efforts and work.

Sharon Drew has excelled in her different careers, including marketing, social work, insurance, public relations, and as a Wall Street stockbroker. In 1984, she started a computer support services company in London. There, she honed her sales and management skills, expanding her company from a one-woman operation to a $5 million company in four years. Travelling between her offices in Stuttgart, Hamburg, and London, she personally produced over 60 per cent of the sales revenue – a success achieved through her ability to create and maintain loyal business relationships over the phone. She has since moved her work forward by addressing the concept of integrity in sales through the new paradigm, Buying Facilitation®.

Sharon Drew has increased sales for diverse corporations of all sizes including IBM, British Telecom, Boston Scientific, Dean Witter Reynolds, Eastman Kodak, E. F. Hutton, General Electric Information Services, Merrill Lynch, The Principal Financial Group, The Union Bank of California, and US West Communications.

Sharon Drew was an early student of NLP in London with such names as Gene Early and Eileen Watkins Seymour. She now lives in Austin, Texas, but intends to commit more time to the UK, where she is finding a more progressive approach to sales. In her words: "I like to work with visionaries."

Issue No. 22 – July 2003

What might have been

I have seen my own ghost; the life that might have been.

I went to a lunch addressed by Richard Bowker, the chairman of the Strategic Rail Authority. He was very impressive and gave the audience hope that at last there was someone capable of sorting out Britain's railways.

I understand that he is 38 years old. For a long time I have been wondering how someone so young could achieve such a high position. During his address I began to think: "At last; someone who is doing what I would do."

Then I began to put the two together. When I was ten years younger than Richard I was starting a job on a much smaller scale that was very similar to what he is doing on a national scale. I won two national awards and one international award for my work. When I was his age I was not only the co-founder of the bus industry's definitive newspaper but the organiser of the conferences through which the Government launched its strategy to privatise and de-regulate the bus industry.

So why am I not the chairman of the SRA?

Well, the first thing is that when I finished my last degree I decided I did *not* want to work in London. Although it is helpful to know what you don't want, it is much more important to determine what you do want. As a result, I launched Brefi Group, building on my experience of the public sector, small business and the management of change in large organisations. This decision has allowed me to work with lots of exciting and creative people. I have worked or done business in ten countries,

47

including two countries in Africa and many of the states in the USA. I have developed a whole range of skills that I would not otherwise have done.

It also allowed me to spend another two decades with a home in rural Wales, before deciding to move back to Birmingham – an exciting new business environment with easy access to London.

I have enjoyed this part of my career, but it has been as an outsider. Would I have enjoyed a conventional career more – working within large organisations? What other people would I have met and what other talents would I have developed? Where would I be now? And where should I go next?

This time, I have tools to help make decisions. I know we should focus on what we want – not what we don't want. I know the criteria for setting a well-formed outcome. We can return to the neurological levels exercise that is so powerful for our clients and which we periodically update for ourselves. We can also use Andrew Halfacre's new workbook *Seven Ways To Figure Out What You Want* and we can arrange a session with Andrew to coach us through it.

As executive coaches, we know the value of working with a facilitator!

Issue No. 23 – August 2003

Listening beats mediation beats litigation

When I walk home from the train I pass the offices of a litigation lawyer. There is a large notice outside listing all the ways in which they can take money off organisations. I am not keen on the compensation culture and as I pass I mutter to myself "Bloody ambulance chasers" and "Trouble makers".

But I have recently experienced the other side of the coin. I have been employing professional services that I have felt have been of poor quality and that have cost me money. There is a temptation to sue. My concern is not to punish, or even to get compensation – though I would like that. My concern is that my complaints were not accepted. What I seek is recognition.

A growing compensation culture in the UK is costing our National Health Service a considerable sum. And yet I often read in the newspaper that litigants are not after money. They say, "I only wanted someone to take my complaints seriously. An apology would have been enough."

Any feedback from customers, clients or patients is a gift – and complaints are *really* valuable, because they signal processes or attitudes that could be improved.

I am starting a vacation today. When I was booking my flight, I had to wait while the manager spent a great deal of time and effort attempting to find an alternative holiday for a family that had booked into a hotel that had been closed down because of an infection in the swimming pool. The holiday company was going to particular trouble to protect next week's holidaymakers. When he

49

finally was able to serve me, I congratulated him on his concern and commitment, and the trouble he was taking.

Less than a week later there was headline news about a large number of people who had been staying at the same hotel and were already starting legal action because they had had their holiday spoilt. I don't know how the holiday company had treated these holidaymakers, but it did seem to me that its customers had decided to sue before it had had time to make any amends to them.

Customer relationship management is a major theme these days. Perhaps it begins with a willingness to listen, to accept that things do sometimes go wrong and, if necessary, to seek help through mediation. It costs a lot less than litigation.

Issue No. 24 – September 2003

Check out your old habits

I have just returned from a wonderful holiday in the sun.

I hope other readers have also had a rest and a change, and are back rejuvenated.

Working on a tan might not be recommended by dermatologists, but it is an excellent way to empty the mind.

The beaches were generally clean and clear of litter – except that in the sand and the dunes there were lots of old cigarette ends. It amazes me that otherwise respectable people will repeatedly and thoughtlessly stub out their cigarettes on the pavement, or even on the dance floor. They would not think of dropping any other form of litter or vandalising property.

So, why cigarette ends?

It occurred to me that before the health fears of nicotine, most cigarettes did not have filters. The nub end was just a few vegetable fibres and some very thin paper. Stub it out under your heel and it broke up and rapidly rotted away.

Unfortunately, with the introduction of filters, which do not rot, the habit has continued and been passed on to following generations. Similar problems occur in developing countries where vegetable packaging has been replaced by paper and plastic.

This is not an unusual experience.

There is a story about the artillery. Just before the gun was fired a soldier would step back a few paces, and then return after the shot. Why? Well the rule book was written in the time of horses and the soldier stepped back

51

to hold the horse's head through the bang – but there had been no horses for several decades!

You might think that such things do not happen these days in civilian life. When I was a transport planner I studied local bus services. One route went into a coal mine, waited for twenty minutes and then drove out. The mine had been closed down two years ago, but the timetable had not been revised.

Similarly, many pieces of research are later disproved or applied in inappropriate circumstances – but by this time they have entered the general consciousness and are taken for granted. For example, we are frequently told in communications courses that content is only a minor part of the message.

7% of meaning is in the words that are spoken.

38% of meaning is the way that the words are said.

55% of meaning is in facial expression.

These figures contain a valuable truth in drawing attention to the contribution of non-verbal information in a message.

However, they are not actually correct for general communication. Note the comment by original researcher Albert Mehrabian: "These equations regarding relative importance of verbal and non-verbal messages were derived from experiments dealing with communications of feelings and attitudes (i.e., like-dislike). Unless a communicator is talking about their feelings or attitudes, these equations are not applicable."

How much of your business or personal behaviour is based on out-dated assumptions or misunderstandings?

It pays to check.

Issue No. 25 – September 2003

Do you see what you expect to see?

During my recent holiday I visited a series of caves. At one point, the guide prepared us to look down into a 20-metre deep cave. It would be very dramatic but we must take great care not to fall down. Gradually, we moved forward towards the parapet. And from a little way back we peered over. Indeed; it was most impressive. Floodlit to show all the colours and shapes of the stone.

I am not a lover of heights and, as I peered over, my heart was a flutter.

The guide said that, to demonstrate how deep it was, she would drop a pebble. She threw the pebble – and the cave disappeared! As we recovered from the shock we noticed that what had seemed a cave was just a large lake. What's more, it was less than a metre deep. Whereas in a draught proof environment the water surface had been perfectly flat like a mirror, as soon as there were ripples the light from the cave *above* got broken up and the reflection was lost.

As I now moved forward right to the edge to look into the water I had absolutely no fear that I might fall over and get wet! What's more, I remembered that when I had first entered this part of the cave I had been surprised to see some water rippling in the distance, and when I first looked into the great chasm I had wondered how it was that we had just walked through a tunnel, which ought to have been where the new cave was.

But I saw what I had been conditioned to expect to see.

How often does our expectation of a situation cloud

our judgement? How much fear and stress is based on what we convince ourselves might happen rather than what actually does happen?

This week I collected some printing from my supplier. They have been very helpful and I took the trouble to point out to them that the front door of the shop was filthy, which let down their otherwise excellent service. "Oh yes," replied the manager. "It's because people put their hands on the glass. It was cleaned this morning." I am pretty sure that when I visited last year, the doorframe had been dirty then. So for a year or more the staff had been cleaning the glass daily without noticing that the handle and frame of the door they came through every morning was ingrained with grease.

We see what we expect to see. And if we see something every day, we probably don't see it at all.

It's almost enough justification to call in an external consultant. It is surprising what we are able to show our clients that has been there for them to see all the time.

Issue No. 26 – September 2003

Decisions are everything

On the face of it, Brefi Group provides a wide range of services. However, the essence of what we do is to help people change the way they make decisions. Everything you or I do is a result of a decision at some level – and much of our work involves helping clients make better decisions, and learn how to make better decisions for themselves in the future.

Decisions can be logical; they can be affected by emotional forces; or they can take place at a muscular level.

Different approaches have different names, and I thought it might be useful to suggest how they fit.

Coaching addresses decision-making at a logical level, whilst taking full account of emotions – emotions can be the barriers to effectiveness or the motivator for success. Coaching involves exploring perceptions of the context in which decisions are made; it tends to focus on the present and the future.

Sometimes emotions interfere to such an extent that an optimal decision, and action to implement it, is prevented. In this case, perhaps, it is necessary to deal with experiences in the past and 'therapy' is relevant.

Inner Game processes, particularly when applied in sport, help the body to make better muscular decisions. This approach helps the body learn for itself by measuring feedback and alerting the muscles to finer distinctions.

And what is mentoring? Very similar in process to coaching, it includes a greater level of personal involvement and transfer of personal experience.

In fact, they are all approaches to helping improve the decision-making process. The greater the range of skills that we have, the more effective we are likely to be with our clients. And this includes identifying the nature of the issue and the most appropriate approach to its solution. Sometimes, however, it will require appointment of a specialist.

Issue No. 27 – September 2003

The impact of a new environment

I have had plenty of reason to think about the impact of environment on other levels in Robert Dilts' Neurological Levels model this week.

The Neurological Levels model helps individuals and teams align their environment, behaviours, competencies, beliefs/values, identity and purpose, challenging them also to consider a higher purpose – whether work-based, family, social or spiritual in which they make a contribution outside the day-to-day demands of life.

This is a really useful model for studying organisations. It can be used for collecting information, identifying lack of congruence between levels or between organisations, for deciding the most effective place for an intervention to achieve change, or for preparing a specification – *e.g.* a job description or mission statement.

During the week we ran a course in consultancy skills, which paid considerable attention to the logical levels as a means of collecting information and assisting in the investigation phase of the consultancy cycle.

I have also spent the weekend moving into our new office in central Birmingham. Clearly, this is a new working environment, but how does it impact on the other levels? Let's combine the editorial this week with some coaching notes and do a standard review of how it will affect me personally:

Environment

The new environment is in a city centre location with new furniture, storage and equipment. As well as being a Brefi Group office, it will be my working environment and I will bring my history with me by hanging a large number of certificates and pictures from our photo gallery – helping to establish and reinforce my 'identity', and generating discussion with clients about different services that we offer.

The office will be in a sociable context, where I can easily meet potential clients and networkers. It will provide excellent facilities for executive coaching.

Our Internet connection will be upgraded to broadband.

Behaviour

The new office will immediately require a series of new behaviours. It is the first time for many years that I have worked more than a short walk from home. Previously, if I was working with American clients, I could return to the office after my evening meal for an additional shift in different time zones. It was also easy to call in at the weekend to catch up. Although I shall have an alternative workstation at home, a city centre office will require greater discipline and improve my work life balance.

Competence

Mixing with commuters and other professionals will help me generate other social skills and stretch my identity. I shall be more inclined to delegate negotiations in London and the regions to our local teams, applying the skills that I expect of clients.

I shall have to learn new skills in managing documents and data as I operate both a laptop and a desktop computer in different locations and transfer my diary and contacts from paper to a PDA. Access to broadband will ensure that I keep in touch with the demands of an ever improving Internet. It will also require me to be even more sensitive to security issues.

Beliefs and values

Whilst continuing to value travelling to projects across the country and overseas, particularly in America, I will begin to place a higher value on local contacts and involvement in a new community. Indeed, the move is based on a belief that even a virtual team needs a prominent base.

There is an opportunity to test a different belief about abundance – that work will 'flow in', as well as there being plenty of work 'out there'; that the less travelling I do, the more work will appear; that focus will achieve a greater critical mass than dispersal.

I strongly believe that the benefits of the work I do flow out from the workplace through families into the community at large. As I commit a greater proportion of my time to one location, I shall be more able to commit to some *pro bono* mentoring. I might even be sufficiently consistent to be able to join a choir and pre-book for theatre and concert performance – fulfilling some of my cultural values.

Identity

Having left Wales after 27 years I am already challenged with becoming an urban/suburban man.

Here is an opportunity for a major change – from an

outsider to an insider – from peripatetic to office-based – from a supplier to a community to a member of a community – from a specialist professional to a fellow professional.

I believe that identity is key driver, so it will be interesting to observe the subtle differences that arise as a result of these changes.

Purpose

Purpose in the logical levels model includes links outside the system and into society. My purpose remains to help individuals and teams to discover and achieve their potential, to bring alignment between who they are and what they do, and thus to improve corporate performance.

I have done this in conjunction with a team of associates who already fulfilled our criteria on appointment. The opening of a new head office is the first stage of a plan to expand our effectiveness through a more formal structure in which we train and coach others to become associates, thus multiplying our impact for congruent change.

Choice of a base in Birmingham, with its excellent road, rail and air connections, also lays the basis for more overseas business.

Perhaps, any of these could have been achieved from a different base in a different location. But the character and balance of the business would be different.

The implication of this review is that the change at the environmental level will lead to changes at the other levels. But, of course, some changes in other levels have been required in order to achieve the change in environment – especially in beliefs, behaviours and competences, just to decide on and implement the new office.

How often do you refer to the Dilts logical levels model when reviewing the impact and management of change?

Issue No. 28 – September 2003

Words and service

I am surprised at some of the slogans that companies have adopted in the UK recently.

One of the major banks has been advertising that it is time to change your bank. Having dealt with them for many years, I had been delighted to change to one of their competitors – but was surprised that they should be encouraging others to follow me.

Another bank has the slogan "because life's complicated enough". After they made me drag my 91-year-old housebound father into their branch (with no parking access) to prove that he was still who he had been throughout his 30 years as a customer, I wondered: "If life's complicated enough, why make it more complicated?"

A sandwich shop advertises "Less bread". Not very encouraging to visit a shop that advertises that it cuts down on a major ingredient in its product.

Perhaps when they thought up these slogans they had a different perception from mine. But if they had tested them by formally attempting to view them from other people's positions they might have detected the ambiguity and avoided the unintended consequences.

Another of our sandwich shops, called Prêt a Manger, has adopted "Passionate about Prêt, People and Food". It sums up what they are all about, and they use it as the basis for their recruitment, management and motivation. That's more like it!

Our coaching note this week describes how the Disney Corporation achieves a consistent level of customer service through many tens of thousands of staff. They work hard at it – and it works. They chose to start with words.

Dick Nunis, Chairman, Walt Disney Attractions says: "If you design, build, operate and maintain with quality, people will take pride in what they do."

This summer I moved from rural Wales to a large English suburban area. In a small market town like Lampeter it is easy to become known and recognised if you are a member of a small population visiting a few shops over many years. I have been most impressed by two businesses in Solihull, where I am now living. In each case I have brought them only very minor business – and yet I have been treated like a member of the family. Always welcomed, always recognised. They are the Royal Bank of Scotland and 'A Plan' Insurance. Further, the staff are always clean and smart.

Last week I moved into an office block in central Birmingham – a small part of a very large area on eight floors. And yet I have been treated by the staff as if I am the only significant tenant and their new friend. The most powerful word for me is 'Richard', and all the staff use it liberally; not only helpful but interested in how I am getting on – even before I moved in they took the trouble to know about and ask about my holiday – that takes real attention to detail. Congratulations to Stonemartin plc.

I take my hat off to the managers of these businesses, which stand out from the herd. I wonder how they achieved a culture of customer service where others have failed? Did they have an explicit service theme? I noticed, for example, that our move into the new offices was highly systematised so that Brefi Group was fully incorporated into Stonemartin's information systems, furniture and IT was correctly installed and staff repeatedly checked with me for satisfaction.

Issue No. 29 – October 2003

Lessons from public speakers

I am a member of various organisations that expose me to visiting public speakers. I learn from their content, and I also model their presentation skills for use when coaching individuals and teams before presentations.

I have noticed that some high profile speakers do not apply the basic rules of answering a question. These are:

- Acknowledge the question, preferably thank the questioner e.g. "Thank you; that is a very interesting/helpful/relevant question."
- Ensure that everyone has heard the question and that you have properly understood its meaning. In most cases this means repeating it and addressing it to the greater meeting.
- Then answer the question, addressing the greater meeting. It is very intimidating as a questioner to have a personal response with sustained eye contact, and for the rest of the meeting it is frustrating to feel ignored. So take trouble to embrace the whole meeting.
- Finally, return attention to the questioner and check that they are content with your treatment.
- Then move on unless it is a situation in which it is reasonable for the same questioner to ask a supplementary.

I have attended a couple of presentations in the last week. Justin Hughes of Mission Excellence is a former Tornado pilot and Deputy Team Leader of The Royal Air Force Aerobatic Team. The 'Red Arrows' practise three times a day, five days a week. After every flight – regard-less of time constraints – the team carries out a debrief. This is a democratic exercise – no name, no rank, no attitude – individuals are referred to by their job titles, and the leader makes the first comments on his personal performance.

Justin's message was that debriefing is the most pow-erful tool for improvement. The process is:

- Start on time (to the second for the Red Arrows).
- Clear the air of mistakes.
- Discuss what went wrong.
- Discuss what went well and why.
- Discuss what went badly and why.
- Summarise with learning points.
- Finish on a high and leave on a positive note.

My experience of organisations is that they rarely debrief. How often does your team have serious struc-tured words together after an event or at the end of a project?

Another speaker was England rugby captain Will Carling, who spoke about leadership. Will was made captain at the young age of 22 and was involved in a major change in the way the English rugby team per-formed. It was interesting to hear how this 22-year-old captain introduced business management practices into a traditional sporting context.

He told us that he wanted to lead the man, not the rugby player. He wanted to understand the man, know what was going on in his life. "Captaincy is not about giving pep talks at half time but about making the prepa-rations and setting the right tone before the match."

When he took over, the team had become accus-tomed to losing and for many players the main objective was not to get dropped from the team. As a result, they had become very risk averse and preferred avoiding the ball to risking making a mistake. He believed strongly in rugby being a team sport, and is not in favour of the "man of the match" approach. Rather, he wanted them to be proud of each other and of the team. His objective was to change the mindset, and he introduced a three-year programme to win the World Cup.

Will told us how he spent time listening rather than telling and introduced upward appraisal so that he could know what they wanted of him, as well as what he wanted of them. He focused on process rather than outcome and concentrated on what people could do rather than the previous approach, which had been to discover people's weaknesses and coach them out of them.

The result was that the players learned the intensity they needed and focused on winning. The improvement in performance was dramatic.

Issue No. 30 – October 2003

Walk the listen

In last week's issue of *CorporateCoach* I described how Will Carling spent time listening to rugby players rather than telling – which had been the practice in the English Rugby team.

In almost every organisation you can be confident that there is one subject about which people complain – communication. And a lot of the problem here is that people don't take the trouble to listen. Often managers do not take the trouble to ask, and some cultures resist hearing what they are told. It is not uncommon to read about large organisations in which whistle-blowers have been ignored, ostracised or even sacked. And yet whistle-blowing is only necessary when healthy communication of serious information is frustrated. If serious misman- agement or fraud is ignored, what is the fate of smaller and personal issues that affect the morale and effective- ness of individuals?

In the mid 1990s I wanted to move into a larger mar- ket and decided that the most exciting challenges were in the UK's National Health Service and in industry. I ap- plied for chief executive posts in several health trusts. One, in particular, was excellently run – and had I got the post, I would have been bored within a year. But others were badly run.

In one case, there were two non-health service appli- cants and we asked to meet some staff before the inter- view in order to obtain some context. This was denied, but we were able to meet some consultants afterwards. This health trust had had three chief executives in the last year, and we were told that we would meet the most difficult consultants.

We were introduced to two consultants in geriatrics. They were not difficult at all – they were just frustrated with the bureaucracy. One of them told me that he had missed a management meeting and as a result his office had been moved into a toilet (actually a converted bedroom with a toilet and wash basin). He said: "I am concerned that if I miss another meeting I will be put into a cupboard." This was a serious statement from a senior medical practitioner. These two 'problem consultants' would have been wholly co-operative and supportive to the management if they had just been spoken to and listened to.

As it happened, I got a job in industry instead and had a roving role amongst international subsidiaries of an engineering company. Having no line management responsibility I was able to talk informally to a wide range of senior managers and directors. Same story in some cases. Creativity and enthusiasm wasted because nobody bothered to ask.

We hear about the technique of "management by walking about". I would like to propose a development: "management by walking about – and listening". Asking questions and listening is what I do for a living. Is it really necessary to bring in a consultant to tap into the genius of your staff, or to find out why they are not performing to their potential? Better to bring us in to teach managers to listen and to review processes for *two way* communication.

In the last issue I talked about how to answer questions at a meeting. This week we start a series on asking questions – but even more important than the question, is genuine curiosity.

Issue No. 31 – October 2003

Doing what you enjoy

I have spent the last three weekends building a pond with my cousin in Derbyshire. This is the fourth pond that I have built, and one of my hobbies.

It has been great fun and I have absolutely been in my element. Put a bricklayer's trowel in my hand and I am on 'cloud nine'. Further, I love digging ditches and a good pond needs a water flow both in and out.

My cousin says that I have missed my vocation as a landscape gardener – or as a plastic surgeon!

Certainly, it has made me think. If I can enjoy this activity so much, should I be taking it into account in my work? This week I have been mentoring a company director – a similar pleasure.

The things that bring me joy and fulfilment involve creativity and making sense of the world – either bringing structure to it or understanding it. My interests, my hobbies and my work are all related to these core areas. I have had careers in transport planning, publishing, management consultancy and as an executive coach. My interests include choral singing, animal husbandry, vegetable gardening, landscape gardening, property development and reading – all congruent.

How does this relate to the work environment? We are at our most creative and most motivated when what we do is related to who we are. This is something we explore with our clients – both individuals and organisations. Who are they and how well do they fit?

I once had a client who complained that his daughter disliked her job. All she wanted to do was to go to dance clubs. I suggested that if she analysed what was really attractive to her in clubbing, she could find a job that, with a better fit, she would find fulfilling – probably related to people and activity. He believed that she should put up with her work if it paid her wages. I disagree.

We spend so much of our time in work that we owe it to ourselves to find a job that we enjoy. So much of the cost of most organisations is in staff costs that employers owe it to themselves to find people who fit the job.

The good news is that my cousin has decided that once the weather improves in the spring, he wants to dig a lake. That is real fun – a return to gardening with a Hymac!

Issue No. 32 – October 2003

Helping people to know you

Having been based in Mid Wales for 28 years, I recently moved my personal office to Birmingham, in England's West Midlands.

Although I was born in Birmingham I have had little direct contact with the city in the recent past.

How, then, to get to know the key decision-makers and get them to recognise me?

Birmingham is a thriving city, multi-cultural, a major national centre for professional services as well as the focus of the British motor industry. It has undergone huge changes over the last decade, with an on-going development plan for the next 20 years, and 50,000 new jobs forecast by 2010. It is also at the centre of the nation's road and rail networks, with an international airport.

Clearly a good centre for an organisation development company.

It has other advantages; the concentrated city centre means that most decision-makers are based within walking distance of my office, and it has a well-organised community of professional and networking organisations.

Before opening here, I was told that if I could meet 500 people I would have met everybody who mattered.

But what about my colleagues based in London? It is too big and too spread out for such an approach.

However, if you can't meet everyone, you can meet some. The secret is to break it down. Focus on what you can achieve, not what you can't.

My philosophy is that you need to attend something three times before you begin to be recognised, and that once you are accepted as part of the community, then you can start to build relationships. So focus and give it time.

In many parts of the world you will find Chambers of Commerce. In the UK we have the Institute of Directors and the Chartered Management Institute. There are professional societies you could join, Women in Business or other special interest societies. There may be organisations to promote trade or relations with other countries?

Is there a business breakfast club in your area? If not, then why not start one? They are very popular here – I could have breakfast with a different group every day of the week, here.

I am not particularly gregarious, but I do like asking questions (most people don't), and I like dancing (most men don't). What are your interests that differentiate you? You may be very tall, have red hair or wear exciting ties. Whatever it is, capitalise on it.

Here are some examples of how people have come up to me in the last ten days:

"I enjoyed your question."

"Hello. You were at the meeting on Wednesday."

"I don't know anyone here, may I speak to you?"

"What's your name? You have been dancing *all* night."

Plus, I was spoken to by someone I had met at a previous meeting, who then introduced me to someone who came up to him – both local influencers. In the last two months I have appeared twice in the 'People' page of the local paper, as the photographers have recognised that I am someone to be noticed!

Meeting people is like a rolling snowball. The more you do it the more progress you will make – suddenly a quantum leap. Remember, the theory of small-world networks claims that we are all linked by a maximum of six degrees of freedom *i.e.* someone you know, knows someone who knows someone who knows someone who knows someone who knows someone you would like to meet – anywhere in the world.

Issue No. 33 – November 2003

Getting your message out

CorporateCoach is part of our publicity strategy. Our target is 20,000 subscribers, world-wide. We expect to pass the 6,000 mark this week. We hope you enjoy it and will pass it on to your colleagues.

We have gained a lot from other organisations, and believe that we can best develop our profile by making a contribution. Apart from what we publish in *Corporate-Coach* we have a large number of free resources on our website, as well as our free training needs analysis.

Our contribution this week is four more situations for asking clean questions. We also launch a new learning resource Imperial plc.

Last week I talked about how networking can help people meet you.

As well as meeting people, networking introduces you to new ideas and techniques. As a coincidence my networking over the last week has brought me in contact with some experts on public relations. I thought you might like to know what they told me.

Richard Haynes recently told a group of lawyers and accountants that they should expect to attend three net-working events a week. This was at a joint meeting of the Institute of Directors and the local chartered accountants – bringing an additional mix into the evening.

He suggested that you should target your activities to:

- develop a profile
- select targets
- research them

- put them on your database
- open the door
- keep in touch

Ian Squires, managing director of Carlton Broadcasting, spoke to the Chamber of Commerce and gave four rules for public relations:

- Have something to say and get it to the person who needs to know.
- Tell the truth (particularly when things go wrong).
- Be in control (you don't know where communications might end up).
- Communication starts at home – with your own employees.

Steve Holden of Haswell Holden recommends that you should aim to use three different media to get your message out.

These could include:

- Advertisements
- Direct mail
- Press releases
- Seminars
- Networking
- Literature
- Directories
- Website

Issue No. 34 – November 2003

No zeds please, we're British

CorporateCoach is written in International English. This causes confusion to some of our readers who write to point out spelling 'errors'; very often the word 'organisation'. In this week's letter, Nancy Chadd draws attention to the difference and recognises the reason.

When I was in the USA earlier this year, I was discussing the situation with my client and said: "The difference between our two nations is the difference between an 'ess' and a 'zed'." It was not until later that I realised that I had fallen into the same trap of ignorance. For, in fact, the difference is between an 'ess' and a 'zee'!

Spelling is only a small detail in the cultural differences between nations – or even between regions. I met someone recently who had moved to Birmingham from London. She said that she could not understand why people kept speaking to her. "I wondered what they were after," she said. In London, commuters, especially, are known for being uncommunicative. Just as Yorkshire people are known for being blunt.

In America there are differences between, say, New Jersey, the Deep South, and the West Coast. There are greater differences between Britain, America, India and Australia.

The trouble for those of us who use an international language is that it does not represent an international mindset. It is easy for us to misread a situation or unintentionally offend someone from another culture.

If an English person goes to France or Japan, they expect people to behave differently and they are more self-conscious because of the language difference and the effort of communication.

We have a saying: "The meaning of the communication is the response it elicits." In other words, successful communication is the responsibility of the sender.

Richard Winfield

Issue No. 35 – November 2003

You are a metaphor of your organisation

As consultants, Brefi Group places a high value on helping clients determine who they are, why they are here,
and what they stand for. A fundamental of leadership is a
congruent organisation in which all the parts share a
vision and fit together in the optimum manner to achieve
the shared objective.

My favourite management book, *Built to Last*,
demonstrates the long-term value of this, and the British
quality standard Investors in People is based on it.

We place equal weight on helping individuals sort
these matters out as we do for organisations. Our objective is to achieve a fit between individuals and their employers. People like to work for organisations whose
values they share. The Disney Corporation told me that
they recruit for values. They don't sack people for performance, but because "we have a values conflict". If the
values are right, many other things can be sorted.

I attended an enjoyable workshop with Deborah
Spence, an accountant who now advises on image. She
told us: "You are a metaphor of your organisation." Organisations place a high value on projecting brand values
in their promotional literature, maybe applying a strict
corporate style to buildings and stationery. But how often
do they have a strict dress code? And, if they have a
"dress down day" or provide corporate entertainment for
their clients do they have strict guidelines on style and
quality for casual wear?

You cannot not make an impression. Image is about
other people's perception of you. And in our behaviour

78

and our dress we indicate the core values of our organisation.

Have a look around. What can you learn about others from their dress and behaviour? And then consider what do they perceive in you? Are you always both smart and 'appropriate' – whether you are a designer or an investment banker?

And if you would like a further challenge, check out your building, car and website with fresh eyes.

Issue No. 36 – November 2003

Taking a customer perspective

This week's editorial is about awareness. My concern is about awareness of the needs and situation of others.

We recently had the opportunity to submit a tender for a management development programme that was very relevant to our particular skills and experience. It looked ideal, but we had learned of it at a late stage and I was concerned about our ability to prepare an appropriate proposal in the short time available. We prefer to work with our potential clients rather than to submit only a written document. I suggested that before going ahead we find out what the competition would be.

A few years ago I was working with an environmental company in California. This company had a team focused on the wood products industry, where they were very successful in winning business. They averaged one win in three on their proposals for this industry, but one in ten on proposals in other industries. As a result they devoted three days of their top team to preparing each proposal for the wood industry and turned out ten proposals a week for all the others. Could it be that they had confused cause and effect? Perhaps they won one in three for quality proposals and a low score for off the shelf proposals. If they were more selective and spent three days on fewer proposals would their hit rate go up and their total wins increase?

This was the basis of my concern last week. What was the point of a mediocre proposal? Was it worth working over the weekend to get a winner.

Imagine my horror when I discovered that the organisation had invited 200 companies to tender and was expecting a 20% response. Clearly I had asked the right question before committing our time.

Consultants have to cover the cost of sales within the fees they earn from jobs they win. This organisation had apparently given no thought to the needs or situation of the companies they had invited to tender. But who is the loser? Most of those who had prepared proposals would have wasted their time. However, the greatest loser is the organisation. They will probably have to choose between some 30-second rate proposals, when they could have built a relationship with three or four suppliers and ended up with a choice of relevant and thoughtful proposals.

It is in our own interest to think through the needs of others and put ourselves in the place of another individual. Many years ago I did some work for Amec, a large civil engineering company. My secretary sent them an invoice. They probably receive hundreds a week. She did not think about how it would be received, so it never occurred to her to provide any evidence of whom or what it was for. We did not get paid on time.

Recently I signed up for a newsletter with a company I wanted to do business with. It required me to complete two lines of address in addition to 'City'. My address only needs one line. When I drew this to their attention, the reply was that if I entered the town name twice, then the software would work. Simple enough. But what do you think was my impression of the customer care I would receive if I bought from them?

In the book review, below, Andrew Halfacre reports on a book by Stuart Wilde on attitudes to money. Just as many people are worried about public speaking, so, many people in Britain are worried about money. Not about shortage of money – but about receiving money. It embarrasses them and can be a real block to success; sales people who lose effectiveness when they reach a certain earnings level; consultants who find difficulty in asking for their fees.

Money is a highly emotional subject involving all sorts of beliefs about self-worth and fairness. Stuart Wilde's books are about abundance and a willingness to accept what comes towards you. It might be better to give than to receive, but if you will not receive graciously, then others cannot give. We live in a time of abundance. Those who refuse to accept can block the flow of abundance to us all. So let go of your inhibitions and accept the gifts that are offered.

Issue No. 37 – December 2003

I failed the bagel test

Last week's issue included a review of *The Trick to money is Having Some*, which is about being open to receiving money. It is a book that I have recently read and, at a recent meeting, Andrew Halfacre and Cliff Edwards had been teasing me about my own willingness to accept gifts.

Last week Andrew and I were walking through London to a meeting with Cliff when a man stepped out waving vouchers. "Would you like a free bagel?" he asked. My instinctive reaction was to say no, and to walk on. Andrew said: "Why not?" took the voucher and was then able to go into a shop up the street and collect his free bagel. By which time, my stomach was rumbling!

A lesson learned the practical way!

This week's book review is full of practical advice. Author Karl George gives you seven tried and tested steps that, if taken, will increase dramatically your chances of success. He concludes by commenting, "Many people are given good advice but the ones who profit from it are those who are prepared to take action." The comments that rang a bell with me concerned keeping a journal to record goals and progress. It is one of those things I have been intending to do for many a year. Another point that kept cropping up in the book was about the value he had gained from people who had been prepared to act as mentors to him.

I was on the train back to London later in the week when a lady opposite was having a 'public' mobile phone conversation. Of course, I could only hear her side of the conversation. At one point she said: "I suppose it is all right as long as you win more than you lose." Sounds logical – but wrong. All experience shows that the winners in life are those who keep losing. They try more, fail more and succeed more. It is not the ratio that matters. It is the net outcome.

Issue No. 38 – December 2003

Where do we go from here?

My friend and past client Jeff Betzoldt was worried about what people would say at his funeral.

We had rented a house at the Colorado ski resort, Aspen, and were spending a few days with the rest of Jeff's staff team considering the future of the company. When we were not mountain biking down black ski slopes, or walking in the forests, we did some real work like considering our own personal aspirations as the foundation for a forthcoming management retreat to develop a vision and mission.

I was reminded of this by Karl George's list in last week's newsletter.

I had asked the team three standard questions:

- What would you do if you knew you were going to die in six months time?
- What would you do if you received a million dollars?
- What would you like people to say about you at your funeral?

These questions are designed to help you identify what you really wish to do with your life. Are you in the right profession/employment? Are you devoting your time to the things that really matter to you?

Jeff had been particularly struck by this last one and kept referring back to it at further meetings.

Previously Jeff had promoted two managers who, after a period, had asked to be returned to their original management roles. Rather than being concerned about the 'failure' of their promotions, Jeff commented on how lucky they were. "At least they have discovered what they don't want to do."

We sometimes hear people say that you never hear anyone on their deathbed saying: "I wish I had spent more time at the office." Maybe. I am concerned that people should not say on their deathbed: "I wish I had discovered earlier in my life that I could have had a much more enjoyable/fulfilling/worthwhile career!"

For me the most difficult question is the first. What would you do if you discovered that you were going to die in six months? I enjoy what I do; I enjoy the people I meet. And I think that what I do is both important and fulfilling. So why would I want to do anything different?

Does that suggest that I have no other aspirations; nothing that I would like to do; nowhere I would like to go; nothing left to achieve? No. But these things would be in the context of the rest of my life – things that I could not only enjoy in the moment but enjoy looking back on. What would be the point if all would be over shortly afterwards?

But then, perhaps in reality I might not go into the office so often, and might get around to going to more concerts or the theatre. There is the purpose of the question. If you are tempted to set new year resolutions in a few weeks, make sure that you know what you want to do – and this time, ensure you achieve it!

Donald Rumsfeld has been criticised for claiming that the problem is that we don't know what we don't know. He referred to "The unknown unknowns – the ones we don't know that we don't know". He is quite right that this is the category that tends to be the difficult ones. This is one of the categories that we, as outside consultants, focus on with clients – whether it is in scenario planning or facilitation.

We experience our own careers through our own experience of our own careers. How then can we evaluate alternatives that we are unaware of?

We have many readers in India and I am always pleased to hear from them. This week we publish an article by Dr S G Bapat about a business in India that takes a different approach. It provides an opportunity to put our own experience into a different perspective.

Issue No. 39 – December 2003

Monkey business

I was talking to Lorna Sheldon this week about presentation skills training. She explained that one of her exercises was to ask her students to prepare a PowerPoint presentation without words. They could use pictures and symbols only.

I was delighted, as my experience is that, powerful as PowerPoint is, it has had a poor effect on many presentations.

I started to think of what I had used when giving presentations and was reminded of a talk I gave to a divisional conference in Atlanta, Georgia, using a stuffed monkey.

Monkeys are an important symbol in discussing delegation and empowerment. Indeed, I gave one of my clients a monkey on a recent assignment. It is so easy, when someone comes into your office with a problem for you to take it on board and agree to solve it. This is known as picking up someone else's monkey: the little problems that effectively stop you from performing at your optimum efficiency. It is well described in Ken Blanchard's excellent book in the One Minute Manager series, which features in our list of core recommendations.

Blanchard describes the four simple rules from the *One Minute Manager* to pass these Monkeys back to the appropriate keeper and reduce the burden on yourself. If you haven't got a monkey to hand, then you can download a flash card. Make it up with two sides so that when you show it to your monkey holder, there is an equivalent set of messages facing you:

> Do you really need me to make this decision?
> Do I need to be involved in this decision?
> What help do you need to make this decision?

Many managers love to get involved in problem solving. It stimulates the mind and demonstrates their 'superior' competence. However, it inhibits learning by junior staff and can lead to a degree of dependence.

Do you have a monkey strategy? How do you decide when and how to share ownership for someone's monkey?

Issue No. 40 – December 2003

Time to ban stress

Like many people across the globe, we shall be taking some time off over the Christmas and New Year holiday period.

This is a time to take a break and reflect, a time to unwind – and, for many people, a time to set resolutions for the New Year.

If, as you step back, you experience a lifting of a burden, a release of stress – or if the opposite and you experience a build up of stress – then perhaps you should review the role of stress in your life.

What is stress? My definition is simple: Stress is a killer. It is also a symptom of something wrong. Frustration, burn-out, low morale, blood pressure, heart attack. You know the signs. Don't accept damaging stress as a necessary part of modern life – nor as a status symbol.

Stress is unacceptable in the workplace. And increasingly this is recognised by governments and courts. You spend so much time at work; you should be able to enjoy it.

According to Georgia Reproductive Specialists, stress has physical and emotional effects on us and can create positive or negative feelings. As a positive influence, stress can help compel us to action; it can result in a new awareness and an exciting new perspective. As a negative influence, it can result in feelings of distrust, rejection, anger, and depression, which in turn can lead to health problems such as headaches, upset stomach, rashes, insomnia, ulcers, high blood pressure, heart disease, and stroke.

Stress is different from pressure; some people thrive on pressure. Stress can arise from too little pressure as well as from too much. As a general rule, stress is a result of being unable to control your environment. In particular, in work terms it can be related to responsibility. Too little responsibility and you are stressed because you are not empowered to make a difference. Too much responsibility and you are unable to make a difference because you lack the skills or the resources.

So stress is a result of poor people management.

The UK's Health and Safety Executive lists six key stress factors:

- The demands of the job.
- The control staff have over how they do their work.
- The support they receive from colleagues and superiors.
- Their relationships with colleagues.
- Whether they understand their roles and responsibilities.
- How far the company consults staff over workplace changes.

In structural engineering, stress tests are run to help forecast the reaction to heavy loads. Perhaps in business we could include stress tests as a means of measuring the cultural health of an organisation.

Here are some tests for you. How often do you:

- Feel irritable?
- Feel restless?
- Feel frustrated at having to wait for something?
- Become easily confused?
- Have memory problems?
- Think about negative things all the time?
- Have marked mood swings?

- Eat too much?
- Eat when you are not hungry?
- Find it difficult to concentrate?
- Not have enough energy to get things done?
- Feel you can't cope?
- Find it hard to make decisions?
- Have emotional outbursts?
- Generally feel upset?

Physical symptoms can include:

- Muscle tension
- Low back pain
- Pains in your shoulders or neck
- Pains in your chest
- Stomach/abdominal pain
- Muscle spasms or nervous tics
- Twitching eyelid
- Unexplained rashes or skin irritations
- Generally itchy skin for no apparent reason
- 'Pounding' or 'racing' of your heart
- Sweaty palms
- Sweating when you are not physically active
- 'Butterflies' in your stomach

If you are suffering from stress, confronting it will improve your life. If others are suffering from stress, confronting it will improve the workplace – and improve the effectiveness of the organisation.

I end with some light relief, a stress-free poem from some schoolchildren.

The Stress-free Workplace in 50 years time

A poem written by pupils at Leechpool Lane School for Roffey Park Management Institute (in 1996)

> The stress-free workplace,
> It really could be true.
> Work and pleasure rolled into one.
> Read on, this could be you.
>
> The main building is the workplace
> The rest is to unwind.
> The gym, the sauna, a restaurant,
> Are pictures in my mind.
>
> The gym a place to workout
> Or badminton if you care,
> A peace garden to wander round
> No noise or hassle there.
>
> A music area to express your thought
> Or to calm any tension.
> What a place this really is,
> I could work there 'till my pension.
>
> A crèche to cater for the tiny tots
> Their every need provided.
> While you go off and do your work
> In caring hands they're guided.
>
> A restaurant to serve delicious meals
> Or even just a snack.
> A bar for drinks or to tell a joke,
> There's nothing here we lack.
>
> A conference room to discuss and plan.
> A table with many places,
> A lecture room to learn things new,
> A theatre full of faces.

The stress free workplace,
It really could be true.
The idea of this is possible.
Your future's here, are you?

Issue No. 41 – January 2004

Awarding honours

Welcome back;. to those of you in the northern hemisphere from a short break, and to those of you further south from a longer break. We hope you are well rested and ready for an exciting and fulfilling year.

In Britain, New Year is one of the times when we award honours for achievement and public service. This year there has been controversy about the process but generally it is a means of recognising people – famous and unknown – who have contributed to national life.

If we were able to award these honours, who would we choose, and why?

I have three nominations. In two cases I am shamed that our nation appears not to have recognised them and in one case I expect that an award will be forthcoming – but it is early days yet.

My first nomination is Richard Noble. Richard could be described as the sort of eccentric that defines Englishness. In 1983 he broke the world land speed record, raising it from 622 miles per hour, which had stood since 1970, to 633 miles per hour. Not content with this he put together a team that in 1997 raised it to 763 mph. Although he managed to get some commercial sponsorship, it was a continual fight to obtain finance, and the record was broken on the proverbial shoe string. Bearing in mind that a complete rugby team has recently been given awards, I therefore nominate his driver on this occasion, Andy Green.

My second nomination is Tim Smit. Tim conceived the idea of an international visitor destination that would feature major climates from different parts of the world in which the plant environment could be shown off.

He found a disused quarry in Cornwall and set about selling the idea, raising £90 million and building the Eden Project.

Into a 50-metre deep crater three of the world's climate zones ('Biomes') have been constructed and planted with over 100,000 plants representing 5,000 species. The Humid Tropics (Rainforests and Oceanic Islands) and the Warm Temperate regions (the Mediterranean, South Africa & California) are contained within the two giant conservatories that have already captured the public imagination.

The third, or 'Roofless Biome', is a Temperate zone that thrives on the climatic advantages that Cornwall has to offer. Here, a fabulous range of plants from India to Chile rub shoulders with the much loved native flora of Cornwall, the Atlantic rainforests, and many more familiar crops.

The whole is run by an educational charitable trust, and has become one of the most popular tourist attractions in the country, attracting 2 million visitors a year. This voluntary achievement is more spectacular when compared with government-sponsored projects like the Millennium Dome and some other Millennium projects which have failed to attract expected visitor numbers.

Creation of this project was a continuous battle against funding budgets, engineering challenges and the weather.

Both Richard Noble's and Tim Smit's achievements are about leadership and man management as well as entrepreneurial and engineering challenge. Maybe they have refused honours out of respect to the rest of their teams but it seems more likely that an honour to these individuals would be seen as recognition for the teams as a whole.

My third nomination is for a young man who is also a television celebrity. However, my regard for him is concerned with education. He is Jamie Oliver, a television chef. Jamie has set up a charity, Cheeky Chops Limited, to open and run a restaurant in London using 15 trainee chefs taken from the unemployment register.

Jamie says: "Being a good cook isn't about being born to it, it's about discovery and growth. Having not been the brightest banana in the bunch myself, I realised that my biggest weapon in life was the determination, enthusiasm, hands-on and 'actions speak louder than words' approach my father taught me, and I wanted to get this across to others, especially those interested in food."

Jamie's progress with his first year group was followed in a television series. His language is certainly not respectable, but what came out was his deep commitment to helping these people grow – and his personal anguish as he learned from his own mistakes how to achieve this. Here is a true human being giving of himself.

Who would you nominate, and why? And when you have made your selections, consider what does that say about you? Have you nominated people who represent what you stand for, or have you chosen people who you admire because they are different from you?

Issue No. 42 – January 2004

Paying it forward

I have long believed in the concept of casting your bread on the waters – what goes around comes around. The more you give, the more you will receive. Hence the many hours that I spend writing *CorporateCoach,* and the free resources on our website.

If there is a choice between believing in abundance or poverty, then I have made my choice.

However, I have been studying two works of fiction to model the concept, and notice one difference.

My friend Cliff Edwards recommended that I should read *The Godfather.* This is a book about power. And one way that the Godfather gets power is by doing favours for people. Unsolicited – out of kindness! The link to power is that he makes sure that the recipient recognises that he/she is receiving a favour and that, maybe, one day that favour will be called in.

In *The Gorillas Want Bananas,* reviewed below, Debbie Jenkins recommends the film Paying It Forward, so we hired the video at Christmas. It is about a young pupil who decides to do three favours for people. Unsolicited – out of kindness. The key here is that he tells the recipients that he/she is receiving a favour and that they should now do three unsolicited favours. This was his way of making a difference in the world.

The theory is to give purpose to your giving by doing it explicitly. (I am not sure how this fits with my belief that charity should be humble and for its own sake.)

However, there is a difference between the two approaches – namely the implied threat of machine gun bullets if you are unwilling to reciprocate when the God-father calls in his favour!!!

There are two controversies in Britain at present. There is a major debate about the funding of universities. And there is much discussion about the trend to out-source back office services to India.

It is good news that developing countries have raised their educational standards such that they can compete in the global economy. It will increase the abundance of the planet, bring wealth to these countries and generate trade with other countries.

However, it sends an important message to countries in the established economies. They cannot continue to rely on the benefits of an educated workforce. They must continue to raise their own standards or find a different business model. Such changes have occurred in the past with large proportions of the population moving out of agriculture, and then out of industry as technology has advanced. In each case, people have been released from traditional jobs to contribute to growth in new areas. This time round it is a combination of education and communications that is driving the change.

British educational policy has been to expand university education to a larger and larger proportion of the population. But this has been at the expense of excellence. Wherever there are resource constraints, there is likely to be a conflict between quantity and quality.

However, if we sacrifice excellence to mediocrity, we will be unable to generate new jobs to replace those exported. Brefi Group is investigating exporting some functions to India. Initially this will create one job in India – and, we hope, ten jobs in Britain. A win–win situation.

This week saw the publication of league tables for schools. This year they reflect 'value added'; the ability of a school to raise the standard of their pupils, rather than to achieve high results. The tables take account of the educational level of pupils when they start school as well as when they leave. The head teacher of one of the top scoring schools was interviewed. How had they achieved their success? They interviewed each pupil to identify potential and, using national benchmarks, the pupil then set targets for his or her achievement that year. School and pupil then worked together to achieve the target.

An appraisal based process that we advocate at work. We at Brefi Group share that school's mission, to help every individual and organisation to discover and achieve their potential.

Issue No. 43 – January 2004

Do you know who you are?

For the first ten years of my career, I was a public transportation planner. During this time I was fortunate enough to have three jobs that enabled me to be at the cutting edge of developments in three different fields. As a result I became a well-known speaker at conferences for transport policy and practice thinkers.

After a break for a master's in management, I launched myself as a management consultant to the bus industry. I noticed a distinct difference in the way that I was treated and raised this at a conference dinner with some colleagues who sold (advanced) ticket machines. "Ah," they said. "You don't realise. You are 'trade' now." And I had thought I was an expert professional!

Later, I co-founded a newsletter on transport policy. Two of us would meet once a month and work through from Friday evening until Sunday night. We had an early computer (pre-dating PCs) with 64k of RAM, no hard drive and disks that were literally floppy. We printed out narrow columns of text on a daisy wheel printer and photo-reduced them on a photocopier. We then cut them up and glued them on to make-up sheets with Pritt Stick, and photocopied them on to A3 sheets for the final document. On the Monday morning I collated, folded and packed the newsletters into plastic bags.

Although we operated in my smart office, we thought of it as a kitchen table operation. Home-made, perhaps, but the content was high quality and we had subscribers worldwide.

Some time later, a well-known transport professor

congratulated my colleague and commented on the '20 staff' that we must employ to produce it! From a kitchen table identity we recognised that we were actually an esteemed international publication.

I had another jolt to my identity recently. In the few months since I moved our headquarters to Birmingham, I have been running a strategy to establish our profile. However, I remained conscious of the comments of my ticket machine salesman.

I was at a meeting with some well-established Birmingham names, one of whom was in my field. But I was not a lead player in the events. Afterwards, as I spoke with the others, I was surprised that not only was I recognised as an accepted member of the local community, but I was also deferred to as an authority. "Gosh," I thought. "They have believed the hype."

Then I stopped to think. I have probably spent more time and money on personal development skills training than everyone else in the room put together. I have probably worked in more countries than everyone else put together. I have probably been involved in more entrepreneurial enterprises than everyone else put together. I am probably older than . . . . No, not that one.

Perhaps their reality was more accurate than mine.

Now they have given me a different perception of my reality I can behave according to a different model.

It pays to know how others see you. They might be right.

Issue No. 44 – February 2004

Seeing is believing

I have been witness to an act of great courage.

Yesterday I went to a concert by the City of Birmingham Symphony Orchestra in Birmingham's Symphony Hall. This is one of Europe's great orchestras in one of its top concert halls. The internationally renowned City of Birmingham Symphony Chorus was conducted by its chorus master, Simon Halsey, who is also Director of the Berlin Radio Choir, European Voices and is consulting Editor to Faber Music. We were treated to a world premiere of two works by Julian Anderson to celebrate the 30th anniversary of the CBSC.

This was no village hall event.

The last work was Fauré's Requiem OP. 48, which features the treble solo '*Pie Jesu*'. On this occasion it was sung by Matthew Horspool.

Matthew is not yet twelve years old. He has been blind since birth.

He was led onto the stage and placed on a chair next to the rostrum. He appeared to be nervous – who wouldn't be – he kept clenching and unclenching his hands, moving his feet, and at times his cassock was trembling. But when his time came, he stood up and he sang. It was a joy to see Simon Halsey leaning over him from his slightly elevated position, gently conducting the whole orchestra to keep time with this courageous young boy. When the concert ended and it was Matthew's turn to bow, there was a great surge of applause.

As I listened, I gazed around the concert hall. This

huge expanse of colour and detail laid out before me, crisp and sharp – I could see it all. No pixels of a bitmap or jpeg image, but infinite detail. I understand that 40% of the brain is devoted to sight. Not only can we see in such richness and detail but we can recall images from way back in our life. As the young would say: "How cool is that?"

This week in Britain we have been subjected to a debate about the BBC, about its public service responsibilities for truth and balance. Given the choice, I would favour balance, for even where there is accuracy there is not necessarily truth. If we are exposed to a variety of opinions and points of view, then we have the opportunity to decipher the truth for ourselves. The reason that I do not watch the television news but devour radio and print is because of the power of the picture. If there is technology to provide a dramatic picture then there is the desire to support a report with dramatic pictures. Not only may these be fleeting and unrepresentative images but they may also be created just for the media. On radio or in print there is less temptation and if the broadcaster is required by 'balance' to provide at least two perceptions, or you read several newspapers, you will get a better appreciation of reality.

They say a picture is worth a thousand words. The right picture can change the world. In a famine or war situation this can be a force for good. But beware; a simplistic summary can mislead.

Issue No. 45 – February 2004

Second chances

My first degree was in civil engineering. The first year was a general engineering course that included electrical engineering. I was not very good at it, and my laboratory bench was often marked out by smoke rising!

When the first year exams approached I had a problem. Hard as I worked at it, I could not understand the resolution of vectors. This is actually a very simple concept by which a vector, which has direction as well as size, is divided into two perpendicular forces. By doing this, various vectors can be combined. It merely requires the use of sines and cosines. I must have learned it at school.

Anyway, it was wasting my time and work on other subjects was suffering. So I gave up and revised everything else, coming back to it when they were complete. Revisiting it, I quickly understood it and passed the exam.

It is just ten years since I qualified as a practitioner of NeuroLinguistic Programming. Since then I have studied with many of the world's leading trainers and it has increasingly become the basis for my consultancy and is a pre-requisite for all our associates. But it might never have been.

The John Seymour Associates NLP practitioner course was in two parts. You had to pass the diploma in order to move on to the rest of the certificate course. And I failed. Horror, horror.

Generally, I am successful (with the exception of electricity) at more academic activities such as exams and interviews. But NLP is about interpersonal relationships – where I was not so good at all. Success at NLP was very important to me and I very much wanted to move on to the next stage.

Fortunately, Michael Neill took two of us to one side and gave us some personal coaching. Suddenly it clicked for me, and I was able to pass and thus qualify for the next stage. Oddly, the problem I had was in using questions to elicit a client's outcome in the positive. It has since been one of the most important tools that I use in my coaching.

And, again, a simple concept – just a mental block. Many thanks to Michael.

So the lesson is that when you come across people who cannot grasp something it might be a simple blockage, rather than sheer stupidity. A little bit of help could be critical. I wonder how many people have gone on to personal greatness as the result of a little help that you gave them?

Issue No. 46 – February 2004

The secret of internal communication

I was talking to someone this week who works for a communications company. They handle public relations, advertising etc. for clients. This lady was complaining that the staff never knew what was going on, and were not involved in management decisions.

The company had a team briefing system and an open door policy. But, nonetheless, there was a sense that "we do not know what is going on".

Some years ago I worked with a chief executive who made tremendous progress in developing a more open management style. Part of this was to tell the staff what was going on. But, what was the response when we held a meeting to brief the managers? Not "Thank you for telling us and keeping us informed", Oh no! It was: "Why did you not tell us earlier?"

This is a typical situation. Truth, news, facts at the top of an organisation are dynamic – they evolve from day to day, and they can be commercially sensitive. If you tell the staff, when do you tell the shareholders? There are legal restrictions on the release of information for a company where the shares are publicly traded.

Managing information can seem a thankless task. And yet, it is very important for its impact on morale.

Many years ago I had someone working for me. He was based in the room next door, but he did not often call in, nor did I on him. I had complete confidence in his judgement that he would know when to ask for advice or authority, or when I should be advised of something.

And this is the key – trust. It is not the behaviour that counts. It is the beliefs and values. If the staff trusts the management to handle information sensitively and to respect the employees' interest in knowing what is going on by keeping them informed when appropriate, then morale will be high and complaints contained.

Another client was a large industrial organisation, where the middle managers were complaining about lack of information. When I asked them what information they themselves passed down, their response about their own staff was: "They don't need to know." We all need to know, though not necessarily in the same detail.

My question this week is what beliefs, values and processes apply in your organisation? And, how do you respond within the freedom that you have? I hope it is not question of the pot calling the kettle black!

Issue No. 47 – February 2004

Great leaps of learning

Just imagine a world in which you would grow up in a permanent struggle for survival, have lots of children and, when your children are off your hands, die exhausted.

Then imagine a world in which you grew up, had children and, when your children were off your hands, you had energy and life for another ten or twenty years – not only you, but your friends, too.

In the second scenario you might spend time thinking about the world and your experience. You might discuss it with your friends. You might make discoveries or develop new ideas. Longevity and leisure contribute to learning.

Just imagine a world in which you never stray more than ten miles from your own village. Then imagine a world in which people are able to travel around their own country and some people even to travel across continents. Knowledge and ideas travel with them.

Just imagine a world in which knowledge was recorded and transmitted by monks copying books by hand with a quill pen. Then consider the invention of the printing press. Many copies of any text can be manufactured and passed to others.

Consider the impact of mass communication, mass travel and satellite broadcasting. Knowledge is let loose and information and ideas can permeate all corners of the world.

Just imagine a world in which regions and nations have their own language. Then imagine a world in which one language becomes dominant.

Now think of the world that we live in. English is spoken widely across the planet and the Internet not only makes knowledge available to anyone but introduces powerful search facilities, e-mail, newsletters and discussion groups. Now ideas can travel instantly and can be developed dynamically as they travel around the world.

We live at an exciting time. We are living longer, travelling more. We are healthier and wealthier. We have access to unprecedented communications. Knowledge is set free of institutional controls and we can learn for ourselves.

We have seen many changes and developments as a direct result of developments in IT and the Internet. But the greatest changes we have yet to meet. For we live at one of the critical stages in history when changes in the political, social and technical environments lead to a great leap of learning.

However, a warning – such times have occurred before. If we look back on great civilisations of the past like Rome, and China, and India, the Aztecs, we realise that not only have these civilisations disappeared, but civilisation itself, and knowledge, have disappeared with them. It seems impossible that knowledge can die. But it did.

As a member of the *CorporateCoach* community, I guess you, too, are committed to learning and development. The example that we set will influence each of the other communities we touch.

May we all be custodians of knowledge and the practice of learning. May we ensure that the organisations we work in are learning organisations.

Issue No. 48 – March 2004

Learning migration

March seems to be a significant day for me to move. In March 1960 I moved out of Birmingham to a suburb, with a new school and my first practical experience of farming. Lots of new learning.

Today, 1ˢᵗ March, is St David's Day, *"Dydd Dewi Sant"*. St David is the patron saint of Wales. On St David's Day 1975, I moved my family to Wales. As we drove in convoy over the Severn Bridge, which divides England from Wales, I reflected on the significance of this move from urban to rural, to a new language. On the same day a new translation of the New Testament was published in Welsh. A major day for the Welsh nation, too!

Having led one of only two projects in Britain investigating the feasibility of futuristic driverless public transport systems, I then moved into the new discipline of county public transport planning, where the most innovative form of transport was a postman driving a minibus. At the same time I moved on to a smallholding with cattle, sheep and pigs.

New skills and talent moved into Wales and huge learnings for me in both rural transport and animal husbandry!

Today, St David's Day 2004, my son leaves Britain for a two-month tour of India and a year in Australia. He has previously worked in America and toured South East Asia. What is he learning from such different cultures?

America is a country that has been enriched by the historical flows of immigration, and the cultural mix of ideas that it creates. Many of the IT immigrants to Silicon Valley came from India. Now India is developing its own IT industry, partly as a result of Indians returning from American universities with experience of the dot com boom.

Australia is a country that is almost entirely populated with immigrants. It seems to be a right of passage for young Australians to spend some time in the UK and, increasingly, for Brits in their 20s to spend a year in Australia – a cultural exchange challenging home grown ideas and fostering international understanding.

But large-scale migration can also appear to threaten the stability of communities. It is a challenge for us all. How should we embrace change; how can we manage globalisation, and how do we celebrate diversity in a world with so many opportunities?

The companies in *Built to Last* survived changing environments by knowing their values and having sufficiently strong roots to be able to embrace change and take opportunities. In the dynamic environment that we now live in, it pays to invest in vision, mission and values! Then we can welcome diversity without fear.

Using language

Some time ago I passed a tramp sitting on a bench in the park. As I passed, he shouted out: "Excuse me, Sir. I don't suppose you could help me ..."

Without any thought, I automatically replied: "No, sorry," and continued on my way.

It occurred to me then that here was a man who needed some sales coaching. He was guaranteed to fail as long as he used that speech pattern. If he had said: "Excuse me, Sir. I am sure that you could help me..."

I would have automatically replied: "Yes." Then, at least, he could have tried to persuade me.

Issue No. 49 – March 2004

Passion and focus

I have just completed six days of learning – four days with John and Robert Dilts on entrepreneurship and two days with Suzi Smith on health and longevity.

An interesting theme emerged with Robert – the difference between passion and enthusiasm. Passion comes from within and enthusiasm relates to projects. I say that I "suffer from enthusiasm". I am enthusiastic about many things that come along. It is a great disincentive to focus and has cost me greatly – and been great fun.

I was struck when Suzi introduced herself. She said: "My passion is for learning and I love to share my learning with others." Mine, too.

Robert Dilts is the developer of the concept of the Neurological Levels, which is a major plank in my consultancy work. The top level is 'purpose'. My purpose is to help individuals and teams in organisations to discover and achieve their potential. The next level is 'identity'. This is more difficult for me. As a process consultant I can apply my processes in any context, and as a coach, I can help in most situations – because the resources are within the client. What I am for you depends on what your needs are. So what is my business identity?

Last month I received an email from Coachville, containing an interview with Deborah Brown-Volkman, author of *Four Steps to Building a Profitable Coaching Practice*. She is strongly in favour of specialisation. She recommended that coaches should pick a niche and specialise. "Once you specialise, it gives you focus and

113

direction," she says. She thinks that coaches are "afraid that if they say, 'I only do this', they're walking away from something, and you are. If you specialise, there are clients you will walk away from, but what's great is that you're walking towards something that's greater. You have that focus and clients will be able to identify you, they'll be able to get what you do. And once people get what you do, they'll hire you."

This was a breakthrough for me. By ignoring many of the things that I can do, I can now build an identity for what I most want to do. No longer need people be confused, and now they will know when and where to recommend me.

So: "Richard Winfield offers strategy consultancy and leadership coaching to help directors, boards and partners achieve successful change."

If you could be known for only one thing, what would it be? And if you were known only for this, would it help people to understand you better, and would it help you fulfil your passion?

Sometimes less means more!

We have been studying longevity. I would like to pay homage to Alistair Cooke, who has been broadcasting his weekly Letter From America for the whole of my life; wisdom and humour condensed into 15 minutes. At the age of 95 he has agreed to retire. What a role model. And what a loss to my Friday evenings.

Issue No. 50 – March 2004

Corporate retreat for one

Practise what you preach. I have just returned from a very enjoyable and highly productive weekend. I have been on a corporate retreat for one!

Normally I facilitate corporate retreats for the management teams of other organisations. I recommend that every team should have an away day or corporate retreat at least once a year, and preferably every six months.

Brefi Group has been making great strides in the last six months but is being held up because the CEO is dithering – decision overload. You know the Biblical saying about first removing the mote from your own eye? Well I set off with my flip chart and pens and facilitated a retreat for myself. When the notes are transcribed the rest of the team can expect lots to read and some productive meetings ahead. At last, they will cry!

It is coming up to six months since we moved our head office to Birmingham and I set out to establish my presence there. Time for a review. Any move consumes great energy, and we combined this one with an upgrade of our IT. And once you buy one thing from Mr Gates, other things no longer work and more has to be purchased, and installed, and re-learned, and trouble shot, etc.

We have also developed a major piece of software for training needs analysis, diagnostics and surveys. The first edition is now active and the basis for major expansion is in place. Look out for announcements later in the year.

We are currently carrying out a major re-design and upgrading of our website which, although very successful, has outgrown its original structure.

And readers will know that I personally am in the middle of a major professional development programme with Robert Dilts, ITS, Richard Bandler and Coachville, running through most of this year.

So a review has been most helpful to clarify and energise, and hotels have some excellent deals at weekends. Of course, when I see a flip chart, I automatically fall into facilitator mode. The option to get away is open to anyone, though I would normally recommend that you take an external facilitator with you.

My long-term development has represented a journey through life and I was most interested that on our study of entrepreneurs a week or so ago, Robert Dilts introduced the concept of Joseph Campbell's Hero's Journey. I thought you would be interested. Notice the role of the guardian – or mentor. Remember that the client is the hero and the coach is the guardian. One of our roles as coaches and consultants is to help clients recognise their own hero's journey and support them on that journey.

In the same week, when looking for books on leadership, I discovered *Synchronicity*, which describes Joe Jaworski's 'hero's journey'. Synchronicity indeed.

Issue No. 51 – March 2004

Creating a service theme

I have been transcribing the flip charts from the one man corporate retreat that I ran for myself last week. It has been very encouraging and several people have commented on how positive my mood seemed this week.

It is useful to have some time just to review and structure the current situation and to think about the future. We are currently re-designing the website to bring it into line with our current activities and to simplify its message and navigation. As part of this, it was useful for the corporate retreat to review our target audience and our offering.

To do this, I used a process for creating a service theme that I learned from the Disney Corporation. It is very simple, and very powerful.

Service Theme

Two principles must govern the service theme:

> The service theme must be adjusted to reflect changes in the product and corporate image of the company.

> The company must be able to deliver upon the theme.

Create your service theme

Keeping your product and core values in mind, what is

the desired image that you would like your employees to project about your organisation? Write some words and phrases that describe this image:

Professional, facilitative, fun, corporate, supportive, international, local, personal.

Now define your product, delivery method and recipients of your product:

What is your product or service?

"We create . . . success."

How do you deliver the product or service?

"By providing . . . strategy consulting, facilitation, executive coaching and training.

To whom do you deliver your product or service?

"For . . . individuals and teams in organisations."

As a result of using this simple process, I produced this simple 'elevator' statement to describe what we are to someone in an elevator in the short time available when travelling between floors.

"Brefi Group is an international change management organisation that helps individuals and teams in organisations become more successful by realising their potential."

Or, for short: "We help organisations realise their potential."

Apart from statements on printed matter and websites, you never know when you might have an opportunity to 'sell' to someone in a very short time. It pays to have your elevator statement rehearsed. Why not try this simple technique for yourself?

There is more about how Disney deals with customer

service below.

I have also been negotiating the programme for a course on leadership through coaching and mentoring. Once again I am able to turn to Disney.

The Disney foundations of leadership model

Dream it - picture the future

Plan it - unleash creativity

Do it - mobilise the team

Stick to it - sustain the progress

Live it - make an impact

Values

Empowerment and partnerships

Innovation and change

Interpersonal skills

Leadership strategy

Being a behaviour

Being a mentor

Being a catalyst

Being a role model

Coaching plays a major part in achieving the level of customer service for which Disney is world famous. I wonder whether it is coincidence, therefore, that this year's CoachVille conference is to be held at Walt Disney World in Florida?

No. 52 – March 2004

Problems of success

This year is the 250 anniversary of the Royal Society of
Arts.

The Society was founded in 1754 by William Shipley,
a painter and social activist. He brought together a group
of individuals to propose a manifesto for Society "to
embolden enterprise, enlarge science, refine arts, improve our manufactures and extend our commerce". The
RSA originated in Rawthmell's coffee house in Covent
Garden, London, and to celebrate the anniversary, the
RSA launched the Coffee House Challenge.

I was honoured to be asked to facilitate the event in
Birmingham in the local Starbucks. Over a period of two
hours some 26 guests discussed "Developing a capable
population" in four groups. Not surprisingly the subjects
that arose were not related to traditional education but
tended towards communication and social skills.

I have for some months been considering what I
would include in a curriculum for young people. I get
frustrated by the ignorance of politicians and the press
and have wondered what teaching in schools would
improve the situation in the future.

One that commonly manifests is a result of not ap-
preciating the significance of price elasticity of demand.
Our railways have grown very successfully since privati-
sation ten years ago. Unfortunately, although we now
have some wonderful new trains and improved frequen-
cies, the growth has been faster than the rail network can
cope with. The public response to overcrowding is to ask

for the fares to be reduced because of the resulting poor quality of service.

This is nonsense. If the price is reduced, patronage will rise and overcrowding will increase. However, if we follow the basic laws of economics and increase the fares, patronage would go down making it more pleasant for the remaining passengers, and the railway companies' earnings would rise – encouraging them to invest more in increasing the capacity.

Unfortunately, what is 'fair' is not necessarily what is sensible.

On Friday I used the new M6 toll road. This is the first commercially funded toll road in Britain and provides a bypass to the heavily congested M6, north of Birmingham. The toll for lorries has been set at £10, which hauliers say is too high, so that they do not use it. There have been outcries in the press that setting the toll at this rate is unfair because it will 'increase' the cost of goods delivered by road and consumers will be penalised. It cannot do so because all the hauliers are doing is to refuse a choice that they previously did not have. Further, the removal of significant numbers of cars at peak periods will reduce the congestion on the old M6 and improve travel times for those who continue to use it.

There is, however, another argument. I know from my training as a highways engineer that the wear and tear on a road is a function of the number of heavy lorries that use it. On a road designed for lorries, cars and light vans have little effect. So, it can be argued, the toll authority is 'cheating' by taking the low cost traffic and leaving the damaging heavy lorries on the government owned road. Perhaps, however, they have calculated that £10 is the cost of damage of a heavy lorry journey.

I think economics is a wonderful subject – it allows us to get to logic behind emotion. As a consultant and coach, part of my job is to challenge easy assumptions. If the press did the same we would have a more mature (and capable) population.

Issue No. 53 – April 2004

A capable population

Last week I mentioned that I had facilitated the Birmingham event for the Royal Society of Arts Coffee House Challenge at which a group of invited guests discussed "Building a Capable Population".

I thought you would be interested in some of the results. Here is an extract of the notes from one of the groups.

Each participant in this group of six came at the issue from a different perspective. One was an educationalist, who lamented the lack of creativity as a learning topic and the received view that competitiveness is a bad trait. Another stressed the importance of diversity – given sharp changes in demographics, the need to ensure everyone achieves towards their true potential. One stressed the pressures of an ageing population which brings not just the need for support but the obligation to be self-supporting and adopt the "lifelong learning" mantra through a number of career changes. One came from a management orientation where a key philosophy is that of the continually improving organisation, peopled by individuals who understand what that means.

The group identified some characteristics of a capable population:

one that showed enthusiasm, a preparedness to take (considered) risks and to embrace innovation;

one that was open-minded, challenging yet showed mutual respect for the other person's views and background;

one that had basic skills of numeracy and literacy and, importantly, was IT literate;

one that balanced the softer skills of creativity, good social and communication skills and an emotional skill, articulated as a "care mindset".

All the participants in this exercise had been invited for their contribution to local society. I was very impressed by the quality of listening and the groups' ability to allow every member to contribute. There was real courtesy and quality interaction and a suggestion afterwards that, rather than formal activities, there is a need just to organise 'discussion opportunities'.

Last week, this weekend and today I have been studying hypnosis with Richard Bandler, so the newsletter was written in advance. Look out for some interesting reports of my experience in future issues.

Issue No. 54 – April 2004

Who do you know who could help?

This weekend has been Easter, in which it is traditional in Britain for people to give chocolate Easter eggs. Last weekend I was on a hypnosis course with Richard Bandler at which some people were treated for chocolate addictions. Overheard on the last day "...and she gave me an Easter egg. Of course, I can't eat chocolate now!" Changes of life can be dramatic!

Also overheard, a couple talking about getting work. The one said to the other " "The trouble with this industry is that it is not what you know that matters, but who you know."

"I quite agree," said the other. "That is why I make it part of my job, to get to meet the people who matter."

Networking is a skill, and an important part of generating work – as well as being a source of new experiences and learning. There was a song in the 1920s which went: "I danced with a man who danced with a girl who danced with the Prince of Wales." It is surprising how few links there are between ourselves and the people we want to meet.

This is the basis of the BNI breakfast network. Although many members of BNI chapters obtain work from other members, the theory is that they should be able to arrange introductions through their wider networks – a neighbour, a customer, a relative's boss, a golfing partner etc.

The theory of Small World Networks proposes that you are only ever six degrees of separation from anybody else on the planet. It was proposed by Professor Steven H

Strogatz and his student, Duncan J Watts, in the June 4 1998, issue of *Nature*. There had been a game based on Kevin Bacon in which actors were connected to one another through their appearances in films with actor Kevin Bacon. This is how it went:

> Think of an actor or actress.
>
> If they have ever been in a film with Kevin Bacon, then they have a Bacon Number of one.
>
> If they have never been in a film with Kevin Bacon but have been in a film with somebody else who has, then they have a Bacon Number of two, and so on. It was discovered that no one who has been in an American film ever has a Bacon Number of greater than four.

The film industry is a network of small worlds – each film community representing a world. It only takes one actor to have been in another film (small world) and there is a link into another network, with lots of actors – who have also been in other films.

The basis of Small World Networks is that we all have large local networks of contacts. But if only one friend has a contact with another local network, then we are connected to all the members of that network by a second degree of separation.

When I explained this to someone once, she scoffed: "Well then, how many degrees of separation do you have from President Bush?" She chose the wrong target because I have worked with the US Department of Defense with people who would know Donald Rumsfeld, who knows President Bush!

The test that I use as an extreme example is a bushman in the Kalahari. But even this is easy. I know people who have met President Mandela, and I am sure he has met representatives of Kalahari bushmen who would have a connection, direct or indirect, with every individual bushman.

It is surprising how easy it is to imagine links that lead to who you want to meet – people who will introduce you to the next person along the chain.

The secret to networking success at BNI is to be very specific about who you want to meet and what you require. So I thought we might do an experiment with the community that reads *CorporateCoach*.

I would like to contact someone who would like to take over responsibility for the Brefi Group customer relationship management programme. As you might imagine, we have several thousand warm contacts who, at some time, will have need of our services. Who do you know who would enjoy managing this process and ensuring that we consult relevant leads on a quarterly basis? They should be based in the UK, and ideally within easy reach of the West Midlands.

Issue No. 55 – April 2004

Basic training

I have had a very pleasant surprise. *The Economist*, a magazine that I devour each week, has started to publish a list of the top book being sold on the six Amazon websites in America, Britain, Canada, France, Germany and Japan. I would have expected that these would be a few top novels and long running personal development titles.

My delight is that number 4 on the list is "*Good to Great: Why some companies make the leap...and others don't*", by Jim Collins. Along with "*Built to Last*" by Collins and Jerry Porras, I consider this one of the core books that every manager should read.

Some books are bought but not read. I would be surprised if many buyers purchase "*Good to Great*" just to leave on their coffee table. If they are genuinely reading it and putting it into action, then we can expect some great improvements in the way companies are run.

I thought you would be interested in something I found stuck on the door of a refrigerator in a roadside restaurant in Jacksboro, Texas. It certainly follows the KISS principle: keep it short and simple.

Basic Training

> If you open it, you close it
> If you turn it on, you turn it off
> If you unlock it, you lock it
> If you break it, you fix it
> If you can't fix it, you get someone who can

If you borrow it, you return it
If you use it, you take care of it
If you make a mess, you clean it up
If you move it, you put it back
If you make a promise, you keep it
If you don't know how it works, don't touch it
If it doesn't concern you, don't mess with it.

I wonder how focused is your company training in comparison?

Issue No. 56 – April 2004

Change of life

Last week I was at a committee meeting of a local society. One of the members, who had been a leading lawyer in the city, commented that he had been retired for eleven months and that he had decided not to make any decisions or commitments until he had been retired for a whole year.

He was wondering whether he should now offer his services to help other people who were nearing retirement. After all "it is a real change of life and you lose your self identity when you retire".

Later in the week I attended a dinner addressed by the former Vice President of the United States, Al Gore. He asked us to think back and put ourselves in his position three years ago. For eight years he had travelled in Air Force Two. Now when he wanted to fly, he had to take his shoes off at security!!

Now that is some change in lifestyle!! From potential president of the world's remaining super power to ordinary citizen.

He reminisced that, soon after the change, he had been travelling along a freeway in a hire car with his wife and had looked in the rear view mirror and wondered what was wrong – he realised that it was the absence of a motorcade. He said that he understood the personal costs of downsizing – after all he had been the very first sacking under the new presidency.

Al Gore has now become a teacher – a visiting professor ("VP; after all I have to keep up appearances."). He is teaching a course on family centred community building. He also has some roles within the IT industry.

The conference I have been attending is on the site of the furnace of a steel works. Twenty years ago it signalled the end of heavy industry in this area. Now it is a modern hotel set in a beautiful canalside setting with trees, commercial, retail, leisure and recreation developments around. The community has learned new skills and the local economy is growing successfully in the new millennium.

The retired lawyer at my committee meeting commented that he had heard that for every year you delay retirement, you shorten your life by three years. I understood him to mean as a result of the pressure of work. Many years ago I heard a similar comment from someone who was definitely not overworked. In this case the argument was that as you became older you lost your ability to adapt to retirement.

In fact there are many major transitions in life these days and few can expect to follow a single career path for their whole working career. The ability to transition is a skill in its own right and is related to an ability to develop new identities or to maintain a personal identity that is unrelated to one's job role. Wise people protect a life outside work and develop interests that will continue into retirement.

Transitions are the sort of events when coaching can be of great benefit. I specialise in the transitions of promotion – from manager to director to chairman, or from associate to partner.

I noticed as I left the committee meeting that all the other members were retired. In fact, these days society relies on the retired community for many voluntary services. Retirement can be as – or more – active as paid employment. The difference is that you have to structure your time for yourself, set your own pace and are able to focus on the contribution that *you* want to make. But

then it *is* possible to do that throughout your career!

If you wish to enjoy life more, and get more out of it, then call in a coach ;-)

Issue No. 57 – May 2004

Watch out for what you measure

We have long known that what gets measured gets done. Unfortunately, under the law of unintended consequences, measurement can also get other things done. In particular, bonus systems can distort performance over time, especially if circumstances and priorities change.

I have recently read of an extreme and serious example. *Fortune Magazine* recently reported a special investigation entitled "Why we are losing the war on cancer (and how to win it)".

The basis of the report was that survival rates from cancer have not significantly changed over the last fifty years. Why is this?

In 1971, when the war on cancer began, 50% of people diagnosed with the disease went on to live for at least five years. Today, 33 years and some $200 billion later, the five-year rate of survival rate is 63%, a modest 13 point gain. Nearly all this gain is as a result of better and earlier detection. Once cancer has spread, however, chances of survival are scarcely better now than they were three decades ago.

The essence of their argument is that we measure the wrong things. Most research is done on animals, and in particular on the growth of cancer cells. Growth rates are easy to measure, and it is easy to get research grants on this basis. Clinical trials depend on measuring the effect of drugs on cancerous cells and the pharmaceutical industry has grown big on the development of drugs that will slow growth.

But what is the real benefit of extending life from

four weeks to six weeks? It is a 50% improvement – but what real value to the patient?

The real target should be in prevention; for two reasons. Quality of life is clearly much better if you never get cancer, than if you survive it for a limited period. But, also significant is the nature of cancer.

The trouble with cancer is that malignant cells can break away from a tumour and settle in another part of the body. This is known as metastasis. By the time tumours are readily detectable the cancer might be all over the body. It is then too late to treat.

According to *Fortune*, "It is not localised tumours that kill people with cancer; it is the process of metastasis – an incredible 90% of the time. Aggressive cells spread to the bones, liver, lungs, brain, or other vital areas, wreaking havoc."

The real progress has been made in cervical cancer and colon cancer, where screening programmes cause action to be taken before 'proper' cancer develops. But how do you measure the effectiveness of intervening *before* something actually happens? Affecting what might have been, rather than what is already identifiable.

So the satisfying measurability of laboratory experiments on animals and cell cultures, compatible with 'good science' has led to a thirty-year focus on the wrong target – one that is unlikely ever to maximise public health. Fighting cancer may raise cash, but preventing cancer, including treating 'healthy' people will save lives.

Surprisingly there is already a significant body of science that can detect likely pre-cancerous signals in the bloodstream. Of course there is less money to be made from screening healthy people than treating sick ones – especially the terminally sick. And there is less juicy research in developing detection methods than in fighting an unwinnable war.

An extreme and worrying example, perhaps. But

how possible is it that there are similar examples in your own organisation where traditional thinking and practice has continued long after it has ceased to be appropriate and where an alternative approach might be significantly more effective?

Beware habitual thinking and the attraction of clean statistics. Often some fuzzy lateral thinking can be a better approach. Listen to the dissenters and mavericks!

Issue No. 58 – May 2004

The Dell way

I have just booked the Brefi Group exhibition stand at the CBI's Annual Conference in November. At the same time I picked up a copy of the organisation's excellent magazine, Business Voice.

There was an interview with Michael Dell, and I marked many places with my highlighters. Here are some extracts:

> "Part of Dell's success lies in its partnership model. By forming strategic partnerships with specialists in areas outside its core expertise, it minimises its outlay on overheads and assets."

> "We have a phrase at Dell: 'Pleased but never satisfied.'"

> "We have a programme called Business Process Improvement, which offers employees in every part of the company an opportunity to study a problem and implement a solution. This past year, we had about 18,000 teams complete BPI projects to improve our processes and save the company money. Our teams consist of employees from manufacturing, finance, marketing, and throughout the company. We generate over $1bn in savings from the BPI program."

> "Our culture is not to complain about issues, but to fix them, improve them, and make them better."

> "If you don't keep things simple and understand who

you are as an organisation, you won't maintain the pace of execution it takes to succeed."

"We are growing our global management team to create the leaders of tomorrow."

"At Dell, innovation doesn't mean things... it means ideas. It means listening to customers and serving their specific needs. It means tailoring products and services to better suit the way customers work and live. It means improving our processes to be more efficient and to provide more value to our customers. It means making things make better sense."

Good sense from the founder of one of the world's top companies.

I was pleased to be able to ask a question of Oliver Letwin, the UK's Shadow Chancellor of the Exchequer, this week. I asked about regulation and was favourably impressed with his detailed reply. Rather than taking the normal politician's position by saying he intended to reduce regulation, he explained how he had studied the culture and system that tended to create excessive regulation. He then explained his proposals for changing the system, to create a disincentive to unnecessary regulations in the future. Not bad for a politician and merchant banker!

If you take the trouble to understand the dynamics of a system, you are less likely to incur the Law of Unintended Consequences.

Issue No. 59 – May 2004

A traditional mission statement

Last week Andrew, Paul, Perry and I thoroughly enjoyed delivering our workshop "Build a Successful Consultancy Practice". Remember, there is a follow-up "Lessons From CoachVille" on 21 June. Keep your diary open.

This week's coaching notes are drawn from Paul's session on target markets.

Much of what we have been thinking about recently has been to do with who we are and what we are about. In other words, vision, mission and values statements. Many people will have come across a traditional Christian prayer attributed to St Francis. I wonder whether you have thought of it as a mission statement?

Lord make me an instrument of your peace:

Where there is hatred let me sow love
Where there is injury, pardon
Where there is doubt, faith
Where there is despair, hope
Where there is darkness, light
Where there is sadness, joy.

O Divine Master, grant that I might not so much seek:
To be consoled, as to console
To be understood, as to understand
To be loved, as to love.

For it is in giving that we receive;
It is in pardoning that we are pardoned

It is in dying that we are born to eternal life.

(I understand that 'dying' means dying to self – in order to be open to others.)

Here is another source that is relevant to leaders today. This one is from verse 17 of the *Tao Te Ching*:

Leaders are best when people scarcely know they exist
Not so good when people obey and acclaim them
Worst when people despise them.
Fail to honour people, they fail to honour you.
But of good leaders, who talk little,
when their work is done, task fulfilled,
people will say: "We have done this ourselves!"

Any other inspirational quotes for leaders in 2004 will be gratefully received.

Issue No. 60 – May 2004

A positive state for learning

We have *CorporateCoach* readers all over the world and I am making some international trips to meet readers and discuss overseas activities.

Last week I was asked to submit a proposal for some presentation skills training. We offer three modules. The first, 'Introduction', is aimed mainly at creating a positive attitude to presenting in public. Participants start by talking one on one, then work in pairs, and then speak to larger groups. In the afternoon they make team presentations. I choose outrageous subjects and the groups respond in kind. We have a lot of fun and everyone goes away looking forward to the next sessions. These are for smaller groups and focus on practical coaching.

Recently I visited a public speaking club, at which members get lots of practice and feedback. They had some very accomplished speakers. There were two of us visitors and we were asked to give a talk to introduce ourselves. In each case we were told words to the effect. "Don't worry. This will be your worst experience. Each occasion in the future will be less bad."

What an example of setting up a negative state! I am sure that their motives were good. Many people are nervous of speaking in public, but there is no benefit in imprinting the fear – even if it is to reassure people that things will get better. It is rather like telling a child not to worry. The dentist has lots of ways of ensuring they don't suffer pain.

I understand that in Japan, when young children have their first lesson on the violin, they and their parents and friends gather. Before they play a note, each child is given a violin to hold and asked to walk out on to the stage. Here they are greeted with rapturous applause. Surely, this creates a more positive attitude to learning!

Issue No. 61 – May 2004

An attitude of attraction

Last weekend I attended the WealthyMind™ workshop given by Kristine and Tim Hallbom.

I had long thought that I must have a negative attitude to money, and this was why I signed up for the workshop. In fact, as I went through all the tests of beliefs and attitudes, I discovered that I did not have any negative attitudes at all. However, I did discover why I have not made as much money as I should have done.

The belief that I discovered was:

"It is honourable to be a virtuous pauper."

Not a useful belief for someone who depends for his living on charging fees for his services! With a belief like that I should return to a salaried life, from which I can do good without having to charge.

I am pleased to report that, as with so many limiting beliefs, the discovery was part of the cure and I have since come up with several more positive beliefs. However, I wonder what suggestions our readers might be able to suggest. Offers welcome.

The workshop included many useful NLP exercises. However, the fundamental presupposition was that wealth can be attracted by an attitude of mind – an openness to opportunities.

I have, therefore, a belief that "I attract response when people know what I want". This has already been proved by the welcome response of readers to my message last week that I shall be visiting various countries during the next few months. I shall be very pleased to meet readers and also organisations with which Brefi Group can build relationships. We are looking for partners who will promote our trainings and act as our local representatives to provide services in their own countries. More details below.

One of the interesting subjects to be discussed at our recent workshop on building a successful business consulting practice was networking. There was a resistance to pure networking events. Indeed, I have given up such events myself. However, based in Birmingham I am able to attend lots of events where I can meet interesting people or hear useful lectures. Many of these stimulate ideas that I discuss in *CorporateCoach*. Before and after these events there are general networking opportunities where like-minded people can meet and build relationships. You learn and you meet – and it is an enjoyable tax deductible occasion too. What could be better? A triple win.

Last week, for instance, I went to hear Sir John Bond, Group Chairman of HSBC. No ideas for the newsletter, but afterwards I had a very interested talk with the principal of a local further education college.

Issue No. 62 – June 2004

A tragic opportunity

Just before I left for the USA last week, I had an email from someone who said that he did not hang out with the CoachVille community.

CoachVille is very much a community, and it is also a dedicated resource for training and developing coaches. This year's conference on the coaching business, with a pre-conference session on corporate coaching, was about what I am currently interested in. So I came.

CoachVille is a phenomenon. Launched by Thomas Leonard, founder of Coach University, to exploit the Internet and smash the cost of coaching, it featured thousands of downloadable resources. As a founder member I paid $78 for life membership, compared with several thousands of dollars for other coaching schools. Later it was free, and still is!!

I was cynical about this mass-produced approach and thought it would be coaching by rote and box ticking. I am trained in NLP and adopt a very flexible exploratory approach to coaching. However, I thought I ought to experience this other approach to expand my flexibility. So I attended a course with Thomas in London. Surprise, surprise, his approach was the same as mine. Process driven and flexible. I learned a lot from him, but not what I had been expecting.

Not long later he died from a heart attack. Thomas *was* CoachVille – a charismatic leader with many followers – but a typical entrepreneurial company without a management structure. It could have been a tragedy.

In fact, Thomas had chosen to leave CoachVille to Dave Buck. Dave referred to himself as a 'solopreneur'. No experience of running a global business. But, not only has he been up to the challenge, but he has avoided the temptation to keep CoachVille as Thomas made it, and has moved it significantly forward.

A tragedy and an opportunity! Thomas was a great innovator and had developed a tremendous resource of material. But there was no structure. Dave Buck has taken it, shaken it and created a new CoachVille where resources are focused in communities. Further, one of the first things he did was to attend the International Coach Federation conference and commit to building a bridge. CoachVille had been inward looking and separatist. Today, Dave told CoachVille members to sign up for other coaching schools and develop their skills.

Anybody who thinks they know what CoachVille is about should re-think. Visit the CoachVille site and explore. And watch out over the next few months. Things are changing.

CoachVille is dedicated to anyone who is interested in learning – to coaches and to potential clients. Brefi Group associates have drawn on CoachVille from its inception and Brefi Group will continue to support this wonderful global resource.

I attracted an upgrade

I mentioned last week that I had let go of the concept of "a virtuous pauper". It seemed to me that a better concept would be that of a virtuous millionaire. I wondered what would be the difference. One thing would be that I would have a certain model of Jaguar car – but that is in my plan anyway and had little emotional impact. Then it occurred to me that I would travel around the world first class or business class. That did have an impact on my state and was a real motivator. So I wondered whether I should just pay the extra now to get the experience and whether that would raise my game.

But my flights to the USA and my tour in July/August were already booked, so it was a matter for the future. Imagine my surprise on checking in at Manchester airport on Monday to discover that I had been allocated seat 3A! At the front in business class – no first class on this flight.

An indication that attraction *does* work. The theory of attraction was raised again at this week's CoachVille conference. More about that later when you attend my next workshop!

More networking

Since this is very much a personal newsletter, it reflects the particular issues that concern us at present. Currently we are interested in practice building and networking – we are running workshops on this subject and are focused on laying the foundation for an expanded associates' scheme.

Networking embraces any activity that involves building or maintaining relationships. You might not be networking for leads or prospects. You could be networking for suppliers/vendors, partners, associates or joint ventures, business opportunities or ideas. Personally, I most enjoy activities that develop my information or ideas bank, help me to understand the world better, and stimulate new business activities.

Issue No. 63 – June 2004

Lance Secretan

This issue of *CorporateCoach* is dedicated to Lance Secretan.

Lance was the closing keynote speaker at the CoachVille Conference last week. Lance is promoting the concept of Higher Ground Leadership, in which leaders aim not to motivate but to inspire. Supported by wonderful slide presentations like those on his website, www.secretan.com, he took us on a compelling journey to discover what great, inspiring leaders have known: their destiny (**why** I am here on Earth), their cause (how I will **be** while I am here and what I will stand for), and their calling (what I will **do** and how I will use my talents and gifts to serve). He calls this their Why-Be-Do. Leaders who have a clear sense of their Why-Be-Do is inspiring. Their very presence and energy inspires; their Why-Be-Do shines, radiates and lifts the hearts of others.

In effect, he takes the traditional vision, mission and values to a new level.

Lance was the CEO of Manpower Limited who, between the ages of 27 and 40, built it into one of the largest employers in the world. Since then he has created the Secretan Center, is a professor of entrepreneurship at two universities and has written 13 books. In addition to his activities as a consultant and speaker, he runs a series of Higher Ground Leadership Retreats for chief executives of major companies.

Higher ground leadership suggests we can engage people by appealing to their hearts and souls. By engaging people on a new level – by honouring, exciting and nourishing their souls – we can give them more than a reason to work: we can give them a passion for work.

Lance has had a major impact on companies in the health care industry. On the night that he spoke to us the Canadian ice hockey team, the Calgary Flames, were on television in a national final. Six months ago, before he was brought in as a coach, they were at the bottom of the league. Lance knows nothing about ice hockey – only about leadership.

Here is an exercise to develop your own Why-Be-Do:

Destiny (Why I am here on Earth)

What, do you believe, are the most serious physical, spiritual, or emotional threats to humanity and our planet (he uses the term "Terrathreats") that, unless reversed, endanger our future?

Cause (How I will Be while I am here – what I will stand for)

What do you believe in? What are your values? How will you lose these to change the world.

Calling (What I will do and how I will use my talents and gifts to serve)

What are your greatest talents? What do you love so much that it fills your heart with joy? Where do your greatest talents and passions intersect?

Here is Lance Secretan's personal Why-Be-Do:

Destiny: To help create a more sustainable and loving planet.

Personal cause: To inspire others to honour the sacredness in all relationships.

Corporate cause: To change the world by reawakening spirit and values in the workplace.

Calling: To lead and serve through my writing, teaching, and speaking.

The process is discussed in detail in his book, *Inspire – What great leaders do.*

Issue No. 64 – June 2004

Asking for money

I continue to savour learnings from my week with CoachVille at Orlando.

I had the privilege of doing a coaching exercise with a wonderful young lady who told me that she was "The Collection Goddess". She could make people feel good about agreeing to pay their debts.

One of the problems that many people suffer when they first go into business is asking for money. The Collection Goddess gave us some advice. Give 21 people a dollar each (I guess £5 would do in the UK), and then later contact them individually to ask for your money back. She chose 21 people because she understands that 21 days is as long as it takes to change a habit.

Brefi Group associate Andrew Halfacre has another exercise for learning to ask for things without embarrassment. Go into a MacDonald's hamburger outlet and ask for a *pizza*. Keep a straight face and ask in the expectation that they will be able to supply you.

Regular readers will know that I have decided to give up believing that it is honourable to be a virtuous pauper. I have had two demonstrations recently of how a respect for one's own earnings has led to a positive outcome.

I have a friend who teaches presentation skills and public speaking. Last year she attended an international conference in Durban, South Africa. She was approached by a group of women from Malawi, saying that they had been impressed by her contribution and wondered whether she would go to Malawi and teach their club. Her reaction was, "But I have to earn a living," and she did not expect to hear from them again.

Some months later, she had a call. These few women, whose club had had only £70 in its coffers, had contacted the main companies in Malawi and set up five days of training for senior executives. Would she now come, and then give two days training to their club. This she has recently done and had a fantastic time. The outcome is that not only did she have her expenses and fees paid, but the local club made a profit of £2,000!

The 'Dream Coach' at Orlando, Marcia Wieder, had a similar story. Marcia is keen to pass on her training to young people. One day she met the head of the Girl Scouts – I think in the ladies' restroom – and they struck up a conversation. A few days later, the lady contacted her and asked whether she would run her programme at the summer camp. Marcia agreed but asked: "Would it be OK if I found a sponsor?" In fact, she obtained sponsorship from a major New York bank. So she did her value based voluntary work and was paid – and, no doubt, the sponsorship might have led to some other benefits for the Girl Scouts.

When I was in Orlando, I purchased a set of CDs for CoachVille's Phoenix Certified Coach Intensive. This was a two-day workshop led by Thomas Leonard and Dave Buck. It is a training that goes through the path to becoming a certified coach, which consists of:

15 coaching proficiencies

15 clarifiers

15 deliverables

15 frameworks and

15 stylepoints

It is a wonderful system. We already have a set of

competencies for management, developed by the Management Charter Initiative, standards for directors and boards developed by the Institute of Directors, and presuppositions and competencies for NLP. I had not previously encountered these CoachVille standards for coaching and welcome them in addition to the ones for coaching and executive coaching from the International Coach Federation.

In September we shall be launching our programme for successful professionals who wish to become successful consultants, incorporating an NLP consultancy practitioner certification. During the summer it is my job to devise or discover a similar set of competencies for consultancy.

By nature and training I am a systems thinker – it is part of my skills set as a consultant. I often notice occasions where systems thinking has not been applied. I was on a course at Henley Management College many years ago. Lunch was a buffet. I was just saying to someone: "Why do the caterers not think and provide the wine at the end of the buffet table rather than at the beginning, which means we have to carry a full glass while we are collecting food?" when someone turned to me and knocked my glass of red wine, spilling it all!

Similarly with the wonderful set of CDs from CoachVille – they all have the same cover on the jewel case, though the CDs themselves are numbered. This means that it is difficult to pick out the next one to play from the total set of eleven. Not consumer friendly. Then I discovered after playing number three that the next one is also three and there is no number four – an own goal, which rather proves my point. Now I have to get a replacement from the other side of the Atlantic. Never mind, it is excellent content.

One of the stories told by Dave Buck at the beginning of the series is of his wonderful working environment – his home, a house on a lake. Recently he had had an injury playing football that included a cracked skull. His doctor had warned him that he would not be able to return to work for many weeks.

Dave asked: "Would it be alright if I just stayed at home and spoke to people on the telephone?"

"Yes, that would be OK," replied the doctor.

"So I can work then," said Dave.

I listened to this and thought – that sounds to me like having a job. Fancy having to be stuck in one place all the time. I love what I do and, in particular, I value the freedom and variety. Having to be tied down to one place at specific regular times would be purgatory for me. However, for many coaches, the attraction is that they can work from home.

We are all different. And one of the advantages of the Brefi Group associates' team is that we have different styles and interests, along with common skills and values.

Issue No. 65 – June 2004

Do less

I have been listening to the CDs that I bought from CoachVille when I was in Orlando. They comprise a two-day presentation by Thomas Leonard and Dave Buck on the 15 clarifiers, proficiencies, deliverables, frameworks, and style points that make up the CoachVille system.

One incident is poignant. Thomas offered himself for some coaching as a demonstration. He explained his situation. On the next day, the end of the workshop, CoachVille would be one-year old. He had been working very hard for that year, and for the two years before the launch. He had promised himself a holiday and had bought a new black four-wheel drive truck to go camping for five weeks.

However, he had committed himself to preparing various materials in the summer and was overwhelmed with his commitments. On previous occasions he had been so busy clearing his desk before a vacation that he had worn himself out and not been able to go away at all.

His statement was for a role play – but appeared to be real. Within a year he was dead from a massive heart attack!

An illuminating and prescient role play.

I once listened to a tape-set about stress. The speaker explained that he had been asked to give a keynote speech about stress. He had spoken for 44 minutes on various topics and the delegates were wondering when he would get to the point. In the 45th minute he said: "To avoid stress – do less," and sat down.

There are many causes of stress, and overwork is one

of them; and many western countries are experiencing a growing culture of hard work and long hours.

One solution is to do less, and others are to be able to pace activity and to learn to unwind. Meditation can help.

I had an experience recently. I love what I do and enjoy social activities through my work. But over the last three months I have been over-committed. With two international conferences and three ongoing courses, I had not expected to obtain lots of work in April and May (in my budgeting I count April as half a month because of Easter). But this year almost every spare day was booked by clients – very nice, of course! Unfortunately courses and conferences tend to include weekends, leading to 12 days before a weekend break. In addition, I had a busy programme of evening networking events.

I noticed that I was getting tired. Eventually I was able to get home at a reasonable time on a Monday evening and mow the lawn after eating. On the Wednesday I was due to go to a public speaking club. However, I decided that even though it would be a pleasant social activity it would be more sensible to go home. This time after my meal I was able to spend half an hour weeding my salads. I felt so much better; it was a learning event.

For me, half an hour pottering in the garden is a life saver and is better relaxation than a whole evening at the theatre or a concert. What is yours? Do you know?

Do you have a strategy in response to signs of stress or overwork? It could save your life.

Issue No. 66 – July 2004

A sense of community

I have noticed an interesting phenomenon over the last few years. I like flags, and in the USA and Wales it is acceptable to fly your national flag. But until recently, if you flew an English, St George's flag, you were likely to be accused of being a member of the National Front – a nationalist, racist political party.

Over the last few weeks there has been a large proportion of the population driving around England with two such flags flying from the roof of their cars. There is football about and it is now more than acceptable to use the English flag to support your team.

In addition, many people, male and female have been walking around in English football shirts. People want to belong to a community.

When I was at school it was normal to wear school uniforms but in the intervening years there has been a reaction against such threats to our individualism. However, some ten years ago I worked on a long contract for National Power at Pembroke Power Station. Our neighbour was a large Texaco oil refinery. Texaco staff were issued with branded jackets, which staff started to wear outside work. Our staff came in complaining that they did not have a uniform and so people did not know who they worked for. The first sprouts of a new mood.

If people want to identify themselves with a community, what are you and your organisation doing to create an identity for your staff? How can you tap this need? And how might it improve morale and staff retention?

Issue No. 67 – July 2004

When to use eye contact

I have been studying the video of Monty Roberts, "Join Up", having previously read his book. It is fascinating how he is able to relate to and attract a wild horse by using body language he has learned from observing mustangs. He can also do it with deer. A key part is the use of eye contact. If he wants to relate to the horse and attract it towards him he must avoid eye contact. Consider; what do most people do when they want to make friends with a horse? They go up to it, look it in the eye and pat it on the nose. Based on what we do with humans, but not correct for horses – omit the eye contact.

I was interested, therefore, when studying relationships last week with Michael Grinder, that he should say that when giving a command (especially to a teenager), we should avoid eye contact. Eye contact is great for relating but bad for managing – it implies the person is a 'bad person'.

He further suggested that if we include a standard action with our command we can soon communicate the command by body language alone – thus reducing the resistance generated by 'being told'. Not only useful with teenagers, he said, but in business meetings too.

However, proper use of eye contact is important. Avoiding eye contact can give an impression of shiftiness. A short eye contact, then looking away, is a component of flirting, attracting someone's attention. A prolonged stare has the opposite effect. The skill is to know when to use eye contact and how long to hold the gaze.

Here is a list from John Bittleston:

- When you meet someone for the first time
- When negotiations and discussions get tricky
- When you have to fire someone
- When you are holding a meeting
- When you are congratulating someone
- Whenever you say goodbye to someone

I have been investigating hotels for my trip to Asia. I can remember ten years ago being impressed that I could arrange my insurance from a car park using my car phone – a heavy box fitted in the boot of the car and wired through to the handset. Now I can arrange hotels and flights, purchase books and investigate all sorts of matters over the Internet – from my office or a coffee shop. Very soon I shall also be able to do it from my car as 3G telephony is rolled out. And soon I shall be able to replace my typing with voice recognition. Already we are using voice over Internet for international communication – huge progress in a decade.

I have been facilitating a major scenario planning exercise for a UK utility. What will technology have to offer in another ten years? More significantly, what processes do you have for ensuring that your organisation manages progress – both opportunities and threats? Are you responding now? What will be the impact on your organisation in three, let alone ten years?

Issue No. 68 – July 2004

Rest, recreation and a good clear out

This week has seen the First Night of the Proms – a major BBC music season from the Albert Hall in London.

A major news feature has been the first use of the recently cleaned organ in the Albert Hall. After one hundred years, it has been dismantled and cleaned. One hundred years of dust muffled the sound and the concern now is that the fresh, clean organ will be too loud and could harm people's ears!

I heard recently that mental decline is caused by a build up of plaque in the brain – waste products and cell detritus that is not cleared a way.

I have always thought in terms of the UK academic calendar, which runs from September to July – the summer break giving a wonderful opportunity for rest and recreation, and then a return to a new start in the autumn. In academic terms this always meant a new class, a more advanced social position, and learning at a higher level.

These days I don't expect to use the holiday period just for rest and recreation, but also for development work that I don't find time for during the busier commercial months. This summer we should finish the redesign of our website and set in place the basis for launching several new products and some new business initiatives. Also, I am spending time meeting companies in other continents with a view to investigating joint ventures. My challenge is to ensure that I do set aside time for a complete break.

If organs and brains build up dust and rubbish, what

about our organisations, our careers, and our personal lives? A complete break is a good investment. Give your subconscious the time and space for a good clear out and an opportunity to process all the ideas you have collected over the last year. You will return refreshed and creative.

Issue No. 69 – September 2004

What are basic values?

Welcome to the 238 readers who have subscribed during our annual summer holiday. We are back publishing every Monday until our next break at Christmas.

Apologies to those readers in the southern hemisphere for whom August is the winter – I know; I have been freezing in Melbourne for a couple of weeks!

Many thanks to those readers who met up with me in Dubai, Mumbai, Singapore, Melbourne and Sydney. It was a joy to meet you and a great help in deciding our strategy for international growth.

Now it is back to work. We have a major scenario planning exercise coming to completion this month and the last module of a year's programme with Robert Dilts. We have lots of new developments in the pipeline, so watch this space for announcements.

And so to the editorial:

In 1969 I travelled with 500 students on an overland expedition to India. On our way out we visited Tehran and were 'chaperoned' by tourist officers, who were reputed to be members of the secret police. On the previous expedition, two years before, one of the party had flown home from Tehran and given a press conference at Heathrow airport, complaining at the way Iranians were treated under the Shah.

On our return trip, having travelled through Afghanistan (which was then an absolutely wonderful country), we were stopped at the Iranian border and accommodated for three days in tents at the government's expense. This was a quarantine exercise while we were each tested for cholera. Political freedom is a basic value – but so is freedom from disease. Iran was the only country on our 13,000 mile journey that took such measures to protect its population.

During the summer I visited Dubai to deliver a course "Management Leaders" to an international audience.

Dubai is a remarkable place that has grown out of a small pearl fishing port as a result of the intelligent investment of oil revenues. Where there were two hotels on the coast there are now seventeen. Dubai already has more tourists than Australia and plans to more than double this number. The old town is surrounded by skyscrapers, the international airport, with the world's third largest duty free business, is undergoing at least its third major expansion scheme and there are large tax and planning free zones such as Media City, Internet City and Knowledge City. They are building holiday and leisure complexes into the Gulf that are so large they can be seen from space, and there are plans over the next ten years for a theme park in which Disneyland could get lost. The place is a remarkable commercial success and 80% of the population are foreign workers who have been attracted to support this phenomenal growth.

However, on the first morning of my course I used half a glass of tap water to take my anti-malaria tablets. Within twenty minutes I had stomach pains and I was ill for ten days. When I enquired, I was told that you cannot drink tap water in Dubai. Here we have major international tourism and a commercial centre, the result of investing many millions of dollars, and yet they have neglected a fundamental value.

During the time that America was counting votes in Florida and deciding whether George W. Bush should be the next president, I was in the USA. I watched a very interesting television programme about Bush's time as governor of Texas. He had instituted tests of literacy and numeracy that were dominating the syllabus of junior schools at the cost of a more balanced education. The debate was about which was more important – the general education of the brighter pupils or the minimum achievements of the many. Which was worse, a syllabus dominated by testing or significant numbers of pupils who failed to achieve basic standards of numeracy and literacy.

I was interested to read last week a report in *The Economist* on a study to measure the impact of the knowledge economy. The question was: "To what extent is economic growth driven by the acquisition of 'human capital'?" The conclusion was that, although higher education was good for the earning capacity of the individual, there was only weak evidence that high or rising completion rates of secondary or university education are associated with a country's long-term growth. However, there was a clear and significant association between literacy, labour productivity and rise in gross domestic product per head. "Raising the basic skills of the whole population can bring tangible macroeconomic gains that can help justify the cost of remedial literacy programmes."

So, what are your basic values? Where should you, your organisation or your government focus effort? Sometimes the activities that make a difference can be quite mundane. We know some companies whose Corporate Social Responsibility programmes include staff visiting schools or adult centres to help with reading practice. Seems like the right priority.

Probably the greatest gifts I have received in life are good health and the ability to read. So let us give thanks for public health officials and teachers.

PS: I am returning to Dubai in December to address a conference on Career Development.

Issue No. 70 – September 2004

The structure of conversation

Many years ago when I was learning Welsh, we were taught apparently superficial sentences, such as "What is your name?" "My name is..." "Where do you live?" "I come from..." I thought it was rather on the level of "The cat sat on the mat" and "Voici la plume de ma tante".

However, some months later I attended a conference for Welsh born and incoming English people like myself. Sitting behind me were a couple having a conversation in Welsh. They were using just the phases and questions that we had studied. "What is your name?" "Where do you come from?" "What do you do?" I realised that there is a structure to social conversation. It could go something like this:

Where do you live/work? Isn't this weather terrible!

What do you do?

What are your particular skills/what are you good at? What is your profession?

What do you believe in/what are some of the things that are important to you? (What might we have in common?)

What role do you play/Who are you being when you are at work/home?

How do you fit into society/how do you contribute/ why are you here?

You might not phrase your conversation exactly like this, but I wonder whether you recognise the structure. It starts very safe with the environment, behaviours and skills/competencies. Then, as you build rapport and trust, moves into deeper areas of beliefs and values, identity and purpose. This is the structure of Robert Dilts' neuro-logical levels.

I use this exercise at the start of a workshop. It helps people get to know each other and demonstrates listen-ing skills. I put people into two lines, preferably sitting down with chairs close together and knees almost touch-ing. Then I ask the people to think of an incident that is 'safe', probably from their youth. Those on one side then have to describe the environment in which it took place to their partner in the other team. The partners must listen – but not speak. Then the partners swap roles. I then get one team to move along one chair. If there is an odd number of people, the spare person stands at one end and watches the interactions. When the team moves along, then the observer is exchanged, so that all are involved.

I then ask the second question: "Please describe what you did, what happened?" Repeat the exercise. Ask the third question: "What skills or talents did you/each side display in this event?"

After the three questions, I stop the exercise and ask for feedback. "How easy was it to just talk?" "How easy was it to listen without interrupting?" "What body lan-guage helped/hindered the exercise?" "What did the observers notice about the activity?" "Did it become easier as you had practice?"

We then return to the exercise with the three final questions: "What beliefs/assumptions applied in this incident/What were your expectations at the time?" "Who were you being during this incident?" "How did this incident/event support or demonstrate your purpose

165

in life?"

The exercise is introduced as a warm up and listening exercise. Then at the end I ask what they thought of the questions and how easy they were to deal with. Finally, I introduce the neurological levels model or just ask them to register the exercise for later reference.

There is a variation taught to me by Gene Early. Instead of two rows, put people into 'stars' of six – three people sitting back to back in a circle and then three more facing them. Rotate around the three places and then move on to another star. This creates more energy in the room.

Issue No. 71 – September 2004

How do you know what you know?

Some years ago we ran a management development course for senior managers. It was an unstructured course based on the principles of self-directed learning. On the Thursday evening, one of the participants rang his wife and told her, "You don't know what you don't know." He was amused to tell us the next day that he thought this the most important learning of the course, but that his wife was unimpressed!

More recently, Donald Rumsfeld was much criticised in the UK for saying something similar. But recognising this fact is a first stage to opening your mind to possibilities.

We have just completed a seven-month scenario planning exercise with a major UK trade body. Several of the comments in the review were that there were no surprises and that there was a consistency across the scenarios. We did in fact know everything that had gone into the scenarios. This was not surprising as the industry had contributed experts to build the database from which the scenarios were selected. The thing about scenario planning is that in retrospect you can see how the outcome developed. The difference from strategic planning is that you cannot attempt to forecast it. However, the development of five scenarios in some detail allows participants and others later to 'experience' the reality at a different level from a technical report. This means that they are more likely to confront them and that they are more likely to plan in strategies for detecting early signs.

A story meant to criticise consultants says that a

167

consultant is someone who will borrow your watch to tell you the time – and then charge you for the information. I often tell this story to new clients and point out that if they were not aware that the watch could tell them the time, did not know how to use it, or just had not bothered to think about the time, then the consultant was indeed providing a service. Our job is not necessarily to bring new information but to help develop awareness. Our objective is to transfer skills/processes to our clients.

One delegate complained that there was nothing new in the scenarios. However, there had been a very long list of recommendations as a result of the exercise. Would these have been generated by a simple strategy meeting?

One of my favourite comments that I heard many years ago goes like this: "What is talent? Talent is – easy to learn and easy to do." If you acquire knowledge simply and easily, you might not notice that you have learned it.

Sometimes, it is not a question of "You don't know what you don't know" but of "You don't realise what you do know".

Readers will know that I am keen to develop our international contacts. Recently, I was able to meet again with Avinash Kirpal of the International Management Institute in India. He recommended an article "How to get out of a rut" by Paul Lemberg, which the author has kindly agreed for me to publish.

Issue No. 72 – September 2004

Would you rather be happy now?

I have met several people this week who have been talking about how they could be happy in the future. My aspiration is to be happy in the present.

Anthony Robbins has a set of questions that he uses to focus on positive outcomes. I thought you might like to see them.

Anthony Robbins' morning power questions

Our life experience is based on what we focus on. The following questions are designed to cause you to experience more happiness, excitement, pride, gratitude, joy, commitment and love every day of your life. Remember, quality questions create a quality life.

Come up with two or three answers to all of these questions and feel fully associated. If you have difficulty discovering an answer, then simply add the word 'could'. Example: "What could I be most happy about in my life now?"

What am I happy about in my life now?
What about that makes me happy? How does that make me feel?

What am I excited about in my life now?
What about that makes me excited? How does that make me feel?

What am I proud about in my life now?

What about that makes me proud? How does that make me feel?

What am I grateful about in my life now?
What about that makes me grateful? How does that make me feel?

What am I enjoying in my life right now?
What about that do I enjoy? How does that make me feel?

What am I committed to in my life right now?
What about that makes me committed? How does that make me feel?

Who do I love? Who loves me?
What about that makes me loving? How does that make me feel?

Evening power questions:

What have I given today?
In what ways have I been a giver today?

What did I learn today?

How has today added to the quality of my life or how can I use today as an investment in my future?

Issue No. 73 – October 2004

Team building

When I got into the lift (elevator) on Friday, there were two youngish males already there. One asked the other why he looked so glum. "We have got this team building thing tonight. Lots of silly games, I expect."

Clearly team building and bonding did not come high on his priority list for a Friday night!

As it happens, we have had more than the normal interest in team building this week – perhaps there is something in the air. People have different ideas of what is involved in team building. Some think it requires people to go out into the woods and get cold and muddy doing physical challenges. Others, that it is just an excuse to have some fun. "It does not matter too much what we do. We just want to get together and have some fun."

In fact, either extreme approach is valid. But the real key is to have a purpose. Brefi Group can run indoor or outdoor team building activities, but whatever is involved we seek to add value. It helps us greatly if clients have decided on a purpose for the event. Although bonding is relevant, there is much more that can be achieved. There are skills involved in team building, and if an organisation often sets up new teams for short-term projects, then learning these skills is important. So one objective can be to learn team building skills.

Teams are groups of people with a purpose. It is difficult to maintain a team unless it has a purpose. So most of our team building activities focus on identifying and exploring purpose, including vision, mission and values. We can use Robert Dilts' neurological levels model for this.

Teams are made up of people – people with personalities. An effective team is not only one in which the members are committed to a shared purpose, but one in which individuals bring a complementary mix of skills and motivations. An effective team is a balanced team and we use various questionnaires for a team effectiveness audit, which then provide an excellent basis for a general discussion of team dynamics.

Different contributions are relevant in different circumstances and an analysis of personalities not only explains why people behave in particular ways, but when particular individuals should play a dominant role and when they should stand back. For example, at the stage when it is urgent to complete a project is it important that the person most concerned by accuracy should be given consideration, or should leadership pass to someone more motivated by action and completion? It all depends; and such discussions help to build an understanding of how a team can perform more effectively. It also generates respect for individuals who might previously have been undervalued.

One thing, though. Team building *should* be fun – but fun with a purpose. Then you will get real value from your time away.

Issue No. 74 – October 2004

Love strategy

I have been thinking about love!

I first came across the love strategy with Anthony Robbins at his first UK Unleash the Power Within seminar many years ago. Then it appeared again with Michael Grinder. I strongly recommend it not only for communication between lovers, parents and children, but also in the workplace.

The love strategy is about how you give and receive motivational feedback. Think about an occasion when someone said or did something that made you feel good.

Was it an action?

Was it a word or phrase?

Was it a tone of voice?

Was it a touch?

If you would like to receive such communication in the future, then perhaps it would be useful to tell others what happened and how it made you feel. Is your response very specific, or would similar actions, words, tones or touches be equally effective?

Now that you have explained to others what works for you, then find out what works for them. Perhaps they have never thought about it; in which case you are helping them to improve the quality of their life.

It might not be appropriate to ask someone specifically about their 'love strategy'; in which case you should observe how they react in different circumstances.

The love strategy is a sophisticated version of metaprograms. Some people respond best to receiving feedback or compliments by visual (including gifts), auditory or kinaesthetic means. Some people prefer lots of attention (stroking); others are more self-referenced and get their motivation from knowing that they are doing well. Some like to achieve targets; others like to avoid failures.

There is no 'one rule' for motivation. However, there is a 'simple rule': find out what someone appreciates and give it to them.

Issue No. 75 – October 2004

Consulting, coaching, facilitation and training

We are in the process of launching a new company to train consultants, and for several months I have been researching and analysing the theory behind what we do.

We claim that we are a change and talent management organisation providing an integrated package of strategy consultancy, facilitation, executive coaching and training designed to improve corporate performance. But can we differentiate between the different processes? This becomes important when we start to transfer these skills to others.

Part of my research has been to read *The Skilled Facilitator* by Roger Schwarz. At Brefi Group we claim that, whatever role we are undertaking, we operate in a facilitative manner, so his comments on facilitation were very interesting to me.

According to Roger Schwarz, a facilitator has no substantive decision-making authority; his/her purpose is to help a group increase its effectiveness by diagnosing and intervening largely on group process and structure.

According to Peter Block, author of Flawless Consulting, you are consulting any time you are trying to change or improve a situation but have no direct control over the implementation; success is for your expertise to be used and your recommendations to be accepted. The consultant's objective is to engage in successful actions that result in people or organisations managing themselves differently. This requires three kinds of skills – technical, interpersonal, and consulting skills.

Here are some thoughts from me:

Consulting is about collecting and analysing information with a view to making a recommendation.

Coaching is about using the process of setting and achieving goals with the client to develop the client's processes for setting and achieving goals. Coaching can be with an individual or with a group.

Facilitation is about managing a process to enable a group to solve a problem – and possibly to develop its process skills as a result.

Training is about the transfer of knowledge or a skill.

A consultant who cannot also coach, facilitate and train is unlikely to see many recommendations implemented – and the purpose of consulting is to achieve change.

I would be very pleased to receive your views on the definitions and distinctions of consulting, coaching, facilitation and training.

We recently held a meeting to plan the launch of our new training business. I wanted to structure the meeting effectively so that we would explore possibilities before getting too involved in details, so I chose to use Robert Dilts' Disney Strategy. Interestingly, we did not have an independent facilitator and we soon got off the track!

Issue No. 76 – October 2004

A matter of time

We were invited this week to a major conference of the water industry, for which we have been leading a scenario planning exercise. One of the speakers asked: "What is the difference between a good farmer and a bad farmer?" The answer: "About a week."

NLP was originally developed by modelling therapists like Milton Erikson, Fritz Perls and Virginia Satir. As a result, many therapy strategies were discovered. I remember a question: "What is the difference between NLP and therapy?" The answer: "About six months."

Certainly, one of our objectives in our business is to achieve speedy results. After all, in business, time is money. Sometimes, however, it can rebound on us. Dependency is good for business – it leads to long-term customers. But it is not our objective!

There is an ongoing debate in the coaching world as to whether the first session should be "on approval". This is an excellent way of building a client relationship – but what if all the issues are successfully addressed in the first session? NLP Coaching is a powerful intervention. When the time is right it can be startlingly fast. When we respond to our clients' expectations we can forget the power of what we offer.

This weekend I have been attending a course "An introduction to New Code NLP" with NLP Academy. It was a revelation in so far as I discovered that I was given new code NLP in my very first course, with John Seymour. But I haven't been aware of it since. But the universe speaks. I was reintroduced to it by Kathleen Alexander of Clever Fox in Melbourne, and then one of the delegates at a workshop with Robert Dilts was reporting a New Code course with great enthusiasm. I thought I should take action.

The first thing that I did was to follow up Kathleen's lead that John Grinder is teaching coaching in the UK; then I discovered that there was an introductory New Code day. Hence my time this weekend.

The basis of New Code as opposed to the original Classic Code is the use of content-free processes and a reliance on the subconscious. As a result, the impact can be very fast.

I was delighted to be reintroduced to the New Code game "The Alphabet Game". I used to have a wall poster of this and have memories of using it many years ago. But somewhere I lost it.

Editor's Note: You can read all about it below the original article on the Brefi Group web site; just type Alphabet Game into the search box.

Issue No. 77 – November 2004

The end of GROW?

I have long been unhappy with the GROW model, but it is so obviously logical that I have not wanted to deny it. But I have been modelling my own successful coaching sessions, and they don't match GROW. So I was really excited to read an email this week from Dave Buck of CoachVille. Dave claims that the idea that coaching is about setting goals and creating accountability is a myth – and has created a service that is almost impossible to sell.

Dave's approach is much more in line with what I do. I explore with the client, as a result of which the client is able to resolve their own issues. We may well set a few well formed outcomes at the end, but we certainly do not start with Goal and work through Reality, Options etc. Perhaps coaching can now grow out of GROW!

I attended the CoachVille conference this year because its theme was about building successful coaching businesses. I was very impressed with what was happening at CoachVille. I had not expected to attend future conferences unless they were particularly relevant to my current interests. However, I am increasingly coming to realise that CoachVille is where it is at. Dave Buck and Thomas Leonard set out to re-invent the coaching profession with the launch of CoachVille in 2001, and it seems that Dave is continuing to do this.

I was recently pleased to entertain Lance Secretan to breakfast and learned that he is Dave's personal coach. Put Lance and Dave together and you do indeed have a powerful combination.

Brefi Group will keep close relations with these and others setting the pace around the world, so leveraging the effectiveness of coaches in the UK and elsewhere.

Issue No. 78 – November 2004

Good luck, bad luck

I have just been reminded of a story that I tell.

Tomorrow we have a stand at the UK Confederation of British Industry conference in Birmingham. It is part of our strategy to raise our profile amongst corporate clients and to build a foundation for the consultants that we train.

It has been a hectic time because it has required us to design new publicity material, including a leaflet that explains Brefi Group's "integrated approach to releasing human potential"; our concept of integrating the processes of consultancy, facilitation, coaching and training to ensure that we can support our clients in the implementation of solutions. The inside of this leaflet is based on a mind map showing how the four activities integrate.

Unfortunately, the printing company printed the inside upside down. On the eve of a major exhibition we have 1,000 faulty leaflets. Rather frustrating – but it means that we can test them this time and then have a free re-print of a revised version for general distribution and use at our next exhibition, HRD 2005 at Olympia in April. Good luck, bad luck?

My next job is to prepare the presentation for my contribution at the 5th Annual Career Development Conference in Dubai in December. I have booked my flights so that I spend a few days after the conference having a rest and investigating the new Knowledge Village. I tried to book my hotel for these extra days on the Internet. I could not complete the booking for my chosen hotel – I think there was a computer fault. In my haste, I booked another one, near the city centre and the gold souk. Then I discovered it is in another city 16 miles away. How frustrating – but it means I will have to concentrate more on a rest, with time on the beach, free from business concerns. Good luck, bad luck?

Here is the story.

A father and his son owned a farm. They did not have many animals, but they did own a horse. One day the horse ran away.

"How terrible, what bad luck," said the neighbours.

"Good luck, bad luck, who knows?" replied the farmer.

Several weeks later the horse returned, bringing with him four wild mares.

"What marvellous luck," said the neighbours.

"Good luck, bad luck, who knows?" replied the farmer.

The son began to learn to ride the wild horses, but one day he was thrown and broke his leg.

"What bad luck," said the neighbours.

"Good luck, bad luck, who knows?" replied the farmer.

The next week the army came to the village to take all the young men to war. The farmer's son was still disabled with his broken leg, so he was spared. "Good luck, bad luck, who knows?"

Issue No. 79 – November 2004

We are the programmer

It continues to surprise me how much I do not know. Earlier in the year I discovered the definitive book on consultancy that had been published twenty years ago, soon after I started consulting.

This week I finally traced references to Pikes Place Fish, which had been mentioned earlier by Robert Dilts. There is a series of books based on it, available in most bookshops, as well as a video. In the same week I received a newsletter with a headline: "We are not the program, we are the programmer." Both had the same message.

Pikes Place Fish market is a real place in Seattle where the staff decided that they might be doing a boring job but they could decide to make it interesting. As a result of introducing fun to their activities and to their relation with their customers, they have become very successful – and world famous.

The book *Fish!*, is a story about Mary Jane, a manager who was promoted to take over a very low morale department doing boring work. It was known as the toxic energy dump! One day at lunch time she strayed into the Pikes Place market and came across the fish stall and its enthusiastic staff. The story is about how she (and they) transformed her department.

Here are her notes of what she learned from the team at the fish stall:

Choose your attitude – The fish guys are aware that they choose their attitude each day. One of the fish guys said: "When you are doing what you are doing, who are you being? Are you being impatient and bored, or are you being world famous? You are going to act differently if you are being world famous." Who do we want to be while we do our work?

Play – The fish guys have fun while they work, and fun is energising. How could we have more fun and create energy?

Make their day – The fish guys include the customers in their good time. They engage their customers in ways that create energy and goodwill. Who are our customers and how can we engage them in a way that will make their day? How could we make each other's days?

Be present – The fish guys are fully present at work. What can they teach us about being present for each other and our customers?

Mary Jane sent out these notes and then asked her team to meet with suggestions.

The book is less than 100 pages of large type and is an easy read. But, like so many of these metaphor stories, it is full of good content.

I have commented before on advertisements that have unintended meanings. One night this week I took my father into the local hospital for a bandage. On the wall was an advertisement that I believe was intended to dissuade you from smoking. Here is what it said:

Quit®

Saving Lives

Not a great motivator for the hospital staff!

I am a mentor for Birmingham Future, an organisation that supports young professionals in Birmingham.

On Friday I attended a dinner addressed by Professor David Clutterbuck on the subject of mentoring. At the end of a serious lecture on coaching and mentoring, he added a slide about how not to do it. I list below David's take on "The Toxic Mentor".

Editor's Note: You can find this article on the Brefi Group website. Type Toxic Mentor into the search box.

Issue No. 80 – November 2004

What do we expect?

I enjoy Sundays. Saturday is my recovery day – washing and shopping, and maybe a film or a play. Sundays I enjoy because they are an opportunity to cook. During the week cooking is time constrained and tends to be meat or fish and two veg. On Sundays we eat at midday and I can spend the morning cooking something more leisurely and adventurous, a stew or a roast, and making soups for the freezer.

I am surprised how many of my male friends are also cooks. It is not what you expect of the pre-new man generation. But cooking, gardening and keeping animals for food are basic 'grounding' activities – they literally bring us down to earth.

This year I have missed a large number of weekends as a result of the many courses I have attended in my year of professional development. Next weekend I shall be with John Grinder refining my coaching skills, but I am delighted that this is the last one booked.

I was struck when we were at the CBI Conference earlier this month that director general Digby Jones announced that this was the first conference that did not include a weekend. He said: "We talk a lot about work/life balance. We thought it was time we did something about it." It is a challenge to those of us who run courses. Should we expect managers to give up time outside the working week?

British railways have a bad reputation. But they have improved dramatically since they were privatised ten years ago. I hear that European railway managers are now turning to our companies as the leaders in the field! However, the legacy of a run down infrastructure and a massive increase in passengers means that our wonderful new rolling stock and ambitious train operating companies are often let down by track failures.

On Friday I travelled to Manchester to meet a favourite client. It was a beautiful day and the autumn light did some wonderful things with the colours in the fields. I was sitting on a stationary train when the driver announced that we were held up by a points failure. There was an alternative route being considered but there was a points failure somewhere along that as well. (I must point out that we were experiencing the first, unseasonal, snow and freezing conditions of the year.) The conductor came through to talk to the passengers. Two ladies were sitting nearby. They said, "We are not disappointed. We are so used to failures that it is what we expect."

What I don't expect is that our new rolling stock should fail – though it too frequently does. A train had failed at Birmingham. No problem. A train arriving at a similar time was actually two trains coupled together. The rear train was closed to passengers and then decoupled from its leader so that it could be released for our use. Excellent solution, though each train might be a little crowded. However, there was a lot of standing around and waiting by the many railway staff. Even after the de-coupling had been completed there was more waiting before we were eventually allowed to board and the train to leave. Now outside its original schedule it would upset the timings of other journeys that needed to share track and the whole problem would snowball.

I wonder whether if such an incident had occurred in Switzerland, where it is expected that trains run absolutely on time, it would have been treated more urgently and dealt with more effectively. It is what you expect.

I understand that FedEx is committed to delivering *every* package overnight. It is a matter of pride. It is what customers and staff expect.

If you expect to succeed you will . . . because you will make sure that you do. If you expect to fail . . .

Issue No. 81 – November 2004

Thanksgiving

Americans have recently celebrated Thanksgiving, and most of us are approaching the end of the year. It is a good time to think over the things that have been important to us, and to give thanks. Recognising the gifts of the past helps to focus on the priorities for the future. Here are a dozen thoughts from me:

1. The Economist. The arrival of this magazine is a high point in my week and it keeps me going throughout the week. It gives me enormous pleasure with its international news, features and clear thinking.

2. I also enjoy Fortune, and read it ahead of The Economist, because it is lighter. It gives me a greater insight into American opinion. It also gave me the idea for this editorial. Stanley Bing's article 20 things I'm thankful for.

3. I am grateful to my subconscious that supplies me every week with something to write to you in CorporateCoach.

4. I am grateful to the readers of CorporateCoach who volunteered to meet me in foreign cities during my overseas tour this summer, and who send in letters to the editor.

5. I am grateful for the opportunities to travel overseas, especially the two invitations to Dubai this year (next one starting on 11 December, if

anyone would like to make contact this time), as well as my more frequent trips to America.

6.   I am grateful to Dave Buck and Lance Secretan for the work they are doing to develop the coaching profession through CoachVille, which was introduced to me on my trip to Orlando in May.

7.   I am grateful to all those who have taught me and allowed me to learn this year, especially Robert and John Dilts, Richard Bandler, John and Michael Grinder, Carmen Bostick St Clair, Tim Halbom and Suzi Smith.

8.   I am grateful to Emirates and American airlines for giving me upgrades to business class and reinforcing my new identity, and to Continental for donating two return tickets to America. Life is abundant indeed!

9.   I am grateful to David our technical director for beavering away all this year developing a powerful new website, and for being sufficiently divorced from our everyday activities to keep us focused on e-commerce potential and return on investment.

10. I am grateful to Michael our new business development director for providing a generative sounding board and stimulating interaction.

11. I am grateful to my two designers, Joe and Chris, who have enabled me to indulge my creative energy in new brochures and web pages.

12. And finally, for this list, I am grateful to my clients and associates for inviting me to share their joy in discovering new options.

Of course, there are many more, both business and

social.

You may be aware that I am currently studying coaching with John Grinder and Carmen Bostick St Clair. You will have to wait another week for my insights from this course. Suffice it to comment at this stage what a joy it is to experience two such different and complementary styles. I have been researching models for consultancy, coaching, facilitation and training. Carmen has developed an excellent model of coaching that fits my style. Watch this space.

I have had a couple of enquiries about activities for teams needing to learn about negotiation. Two of our downloadable products that I have recommended are Prisoners' Dilemma and the Spaceship Shortlist.

Issue No. 82 – December 2004

Disambiguation

I am a transport representative with the professional services organisation Birmingham Forward and, as such, have been investigating various forms of public transport. Earlier in the year I tried the London 'bendibuses' and as a result no longer use the Underground to get to Trafalgar Square or Westminster. Travelling back from our seminar on Friday I was delighted to note that the bus driver was acting as a tour operator and giving us a commentary on the route and the attractions to be found at the next bus stops. He said that this helped him concentrate on the traffic and made his job much more enjoyable. Another example of how we can take responsibility for making our own life enjoyable.

I learned a new word this week: 'disambiguate'. It was used several times by John Grinder on the coaching course that he was teaching. Remember it if you are playing Scrabble over the holiday period.

Two key lessons I learned in the course:

The benefit of working with someone with a very different style. John and Carmen Bostic St Clair never appeared in the room at the same time but their styles were absolutely complementary and Carmen's contribution gave me the structure I was seeking. In particular, she introduced a strategy for coaching that reflects my own behaviour – which the GROW model does not.

I also learned how much NLP I have forgotten in the last ten years and what an excellent grounding I received from John Seymour.

I came away with lots of revision and further work to

do.

Next week I shall be sending *Corporate-Coach* from Dubai. If any reader would like to meet me in Dubai on Saturday, Sunday or Wednesday, please drop me a line.

Issue No. 83 – December 2004

Getting ready for next year

Our readers in the southern hemisphere are preparing for their annual holiday and many of us in the north are also expecting a short break before the New Year. New Year is a time for making resolutions. I thought it would be useful to set you thinking about what you would like to achieve next year so that, when the time comes, your subconscious has done a lot of the preparation.

I have been picking up messages this year about how visualisation and goal setting can be explained by quantum theory, and I have just been introduced to a book that seeks to explain the relationship. It is certainly a challenge, with its concept that we live in an infinite number of realities. However, there is plenty of evidence that applying the practical approach really does work, whatever the theory. It is an easy read and I recommend *Success Engineering* by Phil Gosling. Indeed, I have bought a special journal in order to act on some of its recommendations.

If you have any doubt about things being the result of a personal visualisation, you should come to Dubai. Just twenty or so years ago it was a small port and fishing town on a large patch of sand. Now it is a major regional centre. Wherever I look from my hotel there are either skyscrapers or cranes. The rate of growth is phenomenal, as is the creativity. Things did not happen here. They were made to happen – a real example of leadership.

It is not just buildings. In spite of the number of large hotels, there is often a shortage of rooms, because so many people want to come here for business, conferences, exhibitions and holidays.

Here is a summary of the approach to goal setting taken in *Success Engineering*:

- Write out your goals.
- Every morning read them out to yourself and visualise them. Feel the buzz.
- Take in an encouraging chapter from one of the many self-development books or audio tapes/CDs available.
- At lunchtime, let yourself go in the 'power' state of deep subconscious conditioning.
- Just before retiring, read out your goals and visualise them.

There are many books available to give similar advice. But there is much more to *Success Engineering* that you will only be able sample if you read it.

Setting goals is fine, but perhaps you do not really know what you want to do with your life. Now is a good season to work through Andrew Halfacre's *7 Ways to Figure out What You Want?*

Andrew is one of our senior associates and I am delighted to include his article on feedback in our coaching tips section, below.

When you know what you want and are ready to do something practical, then you need to set a goal.

Here is an extract from *Clever News*, edited by Kathleen Alexander in Australia. Setting well-formed outcomes is one of the most valuable processes in coaching so I am happy to publish a slightly different version from the one I use.

Well-formed outcomes set the scene for the game plan and allow you to map out your steps whilst considering different angles. It precedes other techniques of goal setting such as writing down goals and visualising.

The seven conditions of a well-formed outcome are:

1. Describe what you want in positive terms. For example, if one of your goals is to "lose 10 lbs", change it to "attain and maintain weight at XXX lbs" (specify your weight at 10 lbs less than current).

2. Is it achievable? Ask yourself if any other human has decreased their weight by 10 lbs. If yes, you meet this criteria.

3. What sensory based evidence will you accept as having reached your target? In other words, what might you see, feel, touch or hear that act as proof. Taking the weight example, this could mean seeing yourself fit into your favourite outfit, looking at your muscle definition in the mirror, imagining how energetic you would feel or hearing yourself being congratulated by friends on your achievement.

4. Is getting the outcome within your control? Getting yourself to the gym to work out is within your control, but getting your partner to do the same isn't. You can encourage them to do so, give them information about the gym, but whether or not they decide to go to the gym is not within your control.

5. Can you accept the cost and consequences of achieving your outcome? Here, consider time, money, the environment and people around you who may be affected.

6. Do you have all the resources needed? This includes your internal and external resources such as skills, beliefs, time, money, expertise, etc. If you don't have the necessary resources, how can you get them?

7. If you could have the outcome now, would you

take it?

Once you have met the above conditions, by all means use other goal setting techniques such as writing down your goals, creating a more detailed action plan and engaging all your senses to imagine what it would be like to achieve your outcome.

I hope the above suggestions will help you achieve compelling outcomes in 2005.

This is the last CorporateCoach this year, so may I take this opportunity to wish all our readers – and contributors – an enjoyable holiday season.

Issue No. 84 – January 2005

What to do when the resolutions fail

Welcome back, and a happy New Year. May I wish all our readers the very best for the New Year, both in terms of personal achievement and success in your organisation.

This is a time conveniently after many people have made New Year resolutions. Is it about the time when they drop the resolutions, or face up to the fact that they were never going to achieve them anyway?

My view is that resolutions are bound to fail. They are a conscious decision to do something that requires a change in the system, especially at a subconscious level. And without a change, the system will fight back.

As Phil Gosling says in *Success Engineering*, "Unless you change what you are, you'll always get what you've got."

One of the advantages of being an executive coach is that in coaching a client you hear yourself giving advice that would be really helpful to yourself – but which you might never think of for yourself. Just such an event occurred last week.

One of my clients wanted to work on his work life balance. More accurately, after two weeks holiday, he realised that what he really needed was to rescue his life. His work was fine. His career was progressing very well. There was just too much of it, and he was only home to sleep. He didn't really have a life.

On the face of it the challenge was to manage his time better and to work more efficiently. Smacked of a New Year's resolution – just try harder.

My perception was that work was going well because

he had a strong vision of what it should be like – there is lots of structure and a long hours' culture. The problem was that he had no equivalent mental model of a home life. I often hear, and experience myself, that after working long hours someone has time off and does not know what to do with it. It takes time to build a routine and develop different expectations.

I tried an exercise I had learned from Mark Forster. I told my client to write nonstop for five minutes about what he would do if he arrived home at the chosen time every evening. This proved to be very interesting (though as the coach I did not need to know what was revealed). The challenge is to get this new experience into the neurology, so that the subconscious knows what to expect and is motivated to make it possible.

There is one constant moment in the working day – when you arrive. Before the phone rings, before you check your emails, maybe when you make a drink, you have a moment of decision. So, my client's task, until we meet again, is to spend five minutes each morning repeating the exercise and writing up a description of what he will do with his new evenings at home.

I face a similar challenge. Last year was a year of investment and restructuring for Brefi Group. Lots of my weekends were sacrificed to attending courses or overseas travel. This year is to be different; building on last year's investment – and a better work life balance. I need a new routine. Can I follow my own advice?

Issue No. 85 – January 2005

Practical goal setting

I have been putting into practice the recommendations of Phil Gosling in *Success Engineering*. It has been very interesting. Nothing that I have written down is new, and yet my thought processes and awareness have significantly changed. Further, being able to write my goals up on a flip chart has also helped in developing strategy for the management team.

Golding says that because the unconscious mind is like a three-year-old genie, instructions must be very specific. In fact, I found something different. My goal is to have activities in Dubai, India, South East Asia and Australia. When I tried to make these specific, I realised that I did not even know which countries would be the base for my activities in South East Asia, let alone what corporate structure I would adopt. However, I had already discovered that if I put Dubai in my timeline, then a structure would evolve naturally. My experience is that it is enough to seed an idea to the subconscious, and that will change filters and attract developments.

I have set goals in four areas: Brefi Group, Personal, Professional and Lifestyle and I take time to ponder on them during the day. I have two exercise books: a working notebook and a smart journal. Whenever possible, ideally daily, I copy my goals from one to the other. Already some of them are evolving, becoming clearer and more specific.

I find that the best way to learn this process is by example, so here are my current goals for the 'public' part of my life.

Brefi Group

Brefi Group is recognised as a successful consultancy that generates excellent profits and delivers generative value to its clients.

Brefi Associates is a community of 100 independent management consultants, coaches and trainers who work closely with other local members and participate in larger assignments where appropriate.

We have activities in Dubai, India, South East Asia and Australia.

We attract and secure strategic alliances with organisations and individuals with values that we share.

Professional

I help individuals and teams in organisations to discover and achieve their potential by helping them to clarify goals and improve communication.

I explore, distil and communicate new concepts, techniques and relationships for the benefit of others.

I am a successful and respected executive coach working with senior people in Birmingham.

I have built a happy and effective team of entrepreneurial managers.

Warning: Golding recommends keeping your goals secret as people are likely to persuade you that they are unreasonable or impossible. Fortunately, I mix with positive people who believe in continuous generative change and will support rather than discourage me!

Issue No. 86 – January 2005

Raising your profile

Stress is a killer. It is also a symptom of something wrong. Frustration, burn-out, low morale, blood pressure, or a heart attack. You know the signs. Don't accept damaging stress as a necessary part of modern life – nor as a status symbol. You spend so much time at work; you should be able to enjoy it.

I have strong feelings about stress, and one of the objectives of the work that we do is to change people's environment so that stress is reduced. In fact, our mission statement, which says that: "We help individuals and teams in organisations discover and achieve their potential so that they can become more effective with less stress," specifically mentions it.

However, that is not why I am featuring an article on stress in this week's coaching notes. The article came to me completely unsolicited. Someone had researched our website and offered it for use in our publication. In return, they get a link to their website. I am pleased to do this when the subject matter is relevant, but normally I publish articles from people whom we know. In this case the subject matter is relevant, though the linked website is not really an information site.

I publish the article as proof that you can raise your profile and get links by sending out quality content to many potential sources. There are even sites where you can publish articles or find articles to fill your own publications.

Other ways of raising your profile include a programme of public speaking. Many organisations hold frequent meetings, for which they need visiting speakers. Make a list of a few subjects on which you can speak for twenty minutes or so, and then circulate it to appropriate organisation secretaries. Just like articles, when thinking about a talk, you must consider what the potential audience would like to hear and find an 'angle' or 'hook' that makes it relevant.

If you are already a good networker, then you will be used to being in audiences. What is it about the best and worst speakers that you could learn from?

I would like to share with you a publicity idea that I learned from David Frey. The key to business building is building a database of relevant people and organisations. Frey's idea is suitable for building local databases; ideal if you wish to build a local coaching or training business.

Identify one or more restaurants where the right type of people meet, and approach the manager. Offer him a joint venture deal. If he will collect business cards, you will donate a meal and drinks for two each month. In the UK that might cost you £100. The restaurant then puts out a container to collect business cards, detailing the offer and noting that the winner will be notified by email.

At the end of the month the restaurant hands over the business cards and you compile a database – which you share. You – or a celebrity – select the winner and then send out an email newsletter announcing this month's winner, and including a photograph of last month's winner enjoying their meal – and any promotional information of your own, together with some news from the restaurant such as next month's offers, specials or wine selection. The restaurateur might even provide an article on choosing wine. You could also include promotions from other local businesses (for a fee), provided that they strengthen rather than detract from the interest of the email. Provided that people can unsubscribe, you could include addresses from previous months as you grow your database. You might even add a three monthly draw for members of the whole list to maintain their involvement.

Issue No. 87 – January 2005

Letting go of the past

In order to learn, you have to be able to unlearn. To be able to move forward, you have to be able to let go of the past. I heard a story many years ago about a grieving ritual, which I believe was in South America. When somebody died, the remaining spouse had to put the body in a sack and carry it around for a week. This was in a hot country and during the week the body would decompose and start to smell. Without any disrespect to the dead person, this exercise greatly accelerated the letting go of the past. By the end of the week, no doubt, it would have been a joy to let go of the loved one, to bury the rotting remains, and to move on into the future. Death, burial and mourning are celebrated in many different ways around the world, but generally there is a ritual to mark the change point and to allow the survivors to move on.

Other rituals celebrate birth, puberty, marriage, etc. Rituals can be valuable in organisations, to mark a change, whether it be promotion of an individual, the beginning or end of a project, or a retirement. Much of my coaching work is with directors who have not yet made the emotional move from manager to director. They need to let go of their previous role, as well as take on a new identity and learn new behaviours.

Issue No. 88 – February 2005

Beliefs

I thought you might be interested to learn how I am getting on with my goal setting (*CorporateCoach* No. 85). Having written out my goals and gradually improved the detail, I have now written each of the 16 goals at the top of a new page. Next stage is to write a commentary below each one – one or more per day – as I consider the current situation, plans and developments. I must admit that I have not opened my journal in the last few days as I have been extremely busy, but this approach allows me to focus on a small number of goals at a time.

We are involved in facilitating changes at a major industrial plant. We often apply Robert Dilts' Logical Levels model. This reviews an organisation in terms of Environment, Behaviour, Competencies, Beliefs & Values, Identity and Purpose. The management have been operating at the environment and behaviour level; we have been facilitating the creation and communication of a vision and set of values. These can be powerful forces for change. After all, why should you change if your behaviour is congruent with your identity? Change the identity and the rest will follow.

I had an interesting experience of a conflict between belief and identity some years ago. I attended a memory course. I have a strong belief that my memory is very poor – and my behaviour supports this. However, I also have a very strong identity as a competitive learner.

On this day (and this day only) my memory skills were excellent and I was able to take my 'proper' position as the best learner in the room!! Once the workshop was over, I reverted to type and my memory deteriorated.

One of the attractions of NLP is that it helps to discover the mental strategy used for simple tasks. For example, I lived in Wales for many years. One year I offered to prepare the hymn sheet for a *'cymanfa ganu'* at our local church. Typing in Welsh is slower than in English. I noticed that I would read a word, speak it internally and then type what I hear. A more efficient way would be to see the word and then type what I see!

I am concerned that I have great difficulty remembering names. When I see a cat, I think 'cat'. The same with a dog and most other 'things'. But, when I see a person, I refer to a chain of associations from which I can eventually work out what their name is. Better to associate the face with the name when I first meet them – but of course I am more concerned with my belief that I cannot remember people's names!

This week's coaching note is on a related topic. Beliefs are powerful things. "Whether you think can or you think you can't, you're probably right" (Henry Ford). So knowing how to change your beliefs is helpful.

Issue No. 89 – February 2005

Learning to flop

My mother had an aunt, Gwen, who very much enjoyed entertaining and all that went with it. When I was young she used to come to stay when we had a party and work away with mother in the kitchen with great energy and enthusiasm. Every so often she would join me in the sitting room and say, "I have come to flop." For half an hour she would sit quietly – or talk busily – then she would return to the kitchen, fully restored.

For many years I worked for myself from home. If I went away for a training or corporate retreat, I would commit myself wholly to my client, working through the day and then being sociable into the evening. Then on my return home, I would notice that for the next couple of days I was really in a trance, just drifting through time. I was re-charging my batteries.

Similarly, in my publishing days I would work round the clock, with odd breaks for sleep to get the newspaper out. Then I would return home for several days of complete rest and recovery.

Ten years ago I took a salaried post doing much what I still do, but working inside an international organisation. As before, I used to organise and deliver training courses and retreats, often involving weekends. But now that I was employed I assumed that it was my duty to turn up for work every day. I soon discovered that this was not really possible.

As we say in Britain, the penny dropped. I was mixing my values. I was expecting to work round the clock for my internal clients – and behave as a five-day a week employee. I realised that this was foolish, and learned to balance my time.

R&R (rest and recreation), are essential to continued effective performance. It is claimed that in the early 1970s when Britain was reduced by power shortages to working a three-day week, output actually went up.

Many organisations in Britain and America are developing a long hours' culture. Not only is this unfair to employees and their families, but it is also counterproductive. But what about those of us who control our own time? It is easy for us to get sucked into deadlines and to-do lists and to lack proper boundaries between home and work.

Healers heal thyselves. Remember my aunt and learn to flop!!

Issue No. 90 – February 2005

What would you do if you didn't have to work?

This weekend the British National Lottery has a roll-over prize of more than £8 million. An obscene amount of money to win, but it raises the question: "What would you do if you didn't have to work?"

In the same week I have been discussing with one of our associates what we would do if we retired. My answer was that I would do exactly what I am doing now. If I didn't have to earn a living I would spend more time travelling to build relationships and strategic alliances, but that is only bringing forward what I do or am planning anyway.

Regular readers will know that we are in the process of launching a major growth strategy for Brefi Group. The foundations are in place and announcements are planned.

So, why the growth strategy? Is it just to make more money? Is there a risk of destroying what we have built up? After all, what could be better than a life in which I meet interesting people in interesting places to do interesting work? I love to learn new things and to travel. So what would I do if I retired? What many people do – travel to see interesting places, to do interesting things and to meet interesting people. Just what I am currently paid to do!

However, there is a risk that becoming hooked on growth and success can create a burden of administration and stress, stopping you from doing what you enjoy.

I had intended to give you a book review this week. For that you will now have to wait. Rather, I was reminded of the story of the Mexican fisherman. I did tell it to you last June, but it is still relevant and I thought I would include it again.

I have been reorganising my office. Takes time and disrupts other things, but definitely worth doing every year or so. So many things that I should really throw out, so many things that I should really file properly – and so many things that I had put aside and then forgotten about. Here's an example from *Fortune* Magazine, March 8, 2004.

The Hay Group carried out a survey to identify the most admired companies in each industry in America and to discover the behaviours that differentiated them from the others. Here is a summary of the percentage in each group that agreed with key statements.

Behaviour	Most admired	Peers
Performance measures are directly tied to our business strategy	92%	79%
We have translated our strategy into clear plans with accountabilities	84%	74%
Roles and responsibilities are sufficiently clear that people know where to go for the information and support they need to do their jobs effectively	81%	74%
Leaders surround themselves with people who will challenge them on their thinking	81%	60%
Decision-making accountabilities and processes are well defined	79%	64%
All the functions critical to our business success are in place	76%	66%
Leaders devote a significant amount of time to hiring and developing talent	67%	48%

How does your organisation compare? And that includes you, even if you are a one-person business.

Issue No. 91 – February 2005

You can learn a lot from metaphor

When doing team building exercises we sometimes ask groups to express themselves in metaphors. What sort of car would be the equivalent of their organisation? If their team were an animal what sort of animal would it be? This can be a very revealing exercise – and even quite staid managers will enter into spirit of the exercise.

However, there is a lot more that can be discovered through metaphor, especially if you are a visiting consultant or coach. Everything you see or hear is likely to have some metaphorical message. Probably an expression of the people who work there or the organisation that employs them. Sometimes the symbols are the result of unrelated suppliers who just happened to specify them – or they are a legacy of the previous tenant. In this case, although they might not be an expression of the organisation, they are still likely to be identified subconsciously – and thus send confusing or misleading messages.

So how do you spot the metaphors? Well, first look around you. What do you see? What is on the walls? If there is nothing much, what message is that? If there are 'motivational' pictures, what message is that, and what subjects are chosen – nature or sport or...? If there are pictures of people, what message is that? If there are pictures of products, what message is that? If there is a picture of the factory, what message is that?

You cannot not communicate. Whatever is around will be received at some level as a message.

Is the environment clean, tidy, crowded, open plan, cubicles, or private offices? Each environment sends a

212

different message. What about people's desks or workstations? Are they tidy or piled high; are they decorated with photographs and drawings of children; are there lots of pot plants? Is it high tech, or cold and efficient?

Is the atmosphere relaxed or stressed; do people take pride in working late?

What do people wear? Is it a dark suit environment, black sweaters, or jeans and T-shirts – they are all expressions of different cultures.

Finally, listen to the language. Is it the language of competition, with sporting metaphors, or battle, with military metaphors? Do people refer to themselves in terms of a family; do they talk about the product or the company as a 'baby', to be nurtured? Is it a language of frustration, of limits, of restrictions – or one of possibility and opportunity?

Very often people are unaware of the messages they are giving out or receiving from their environment and it is one of the roles of an outside consultant or coach to draw attention to the metaphors and check whether they are truly representative, whether they are helpful and whether different ones could start to generate changes for the better.

And what about yourself? What are the metaphors of your life?

My office has large bookcases, certificates and pictures on the wall and piles of papers on several desks. My colleague Andrew says: "Clearly an academic."

And have you identified a metaphor for yourself – or several? I am an explorer – I like to visit new places, new cultures and learn new ideas and concepts. In the past, I have been a shepherd, both literally keeping sheep and metaphorically referring to my in-house clients as 'my flock'.

So, look, listen and interpret – and you could learn quite a lot.

Issue No. 92 – March 2005

Spring – a time of change

Dave Buck of CoachVille emphasises the difference between procrastination and gestation. Very often things take time to develop and it might be foolish to try to launch them before they are ready.

What is more, it is often the underground, invisible things that are the most important.

Many years ago I was in the room when Nicholas Edwards, the then Secretary of State for Wales, announced his vision for Cardiff Docks. There was great enthusiasm and both the county planning officer and the city planning officer lent their support. For many years it appeared that nothing was happening. But during that time ideas were being developed, people were being influenced and policies and budgets were being passed in public and private organisations. Then there was the major exercise of purchasing land.

Eventually, demolition started, and now South Cardiff is an exciting residential, commercial and recreation area with a new international concert hall. But the most valuable work was done when nothing seemed to be going on.

Spring is coming in the northern hemisphere. Last week we celebrated St David's Day. St David, *Dewi Sant*, is the patron saint of Wales and his day is celebrated with daffodils, which burst into flower at this time of the year. Things are a changing. March is a remarkable month in this country. I used to have a farm. At the beginning of the month many parts of the land would be a stable liquid mud. Then suddenly in about a week, it would change completely to firm ground. We would let the cattle out, and they would dance around in their new freedom.

Soon it is time for digging and buying seeds. The sun shines and people become enthusiastic. Time to set things in motion.

For many organisations it is also the time to be putting to bed last year's financial accounts and setting in motion plans for the next financial year's activities.

Before the days of vacuum cleaners and central heating, this was the time for 'spring cleaning' when carpets were taken outside for a good beating, curtains washed and houses cleaned thoroughly.

It is easy in a modern urban world to lose touch with the seasons but, just as there can be rhythm through the day, a rhythm through the year can ensure that people are refreshed and rejuvenated, practices are reviewed and new ideas brought to fruition.

Many of the best developments may have a long gestation. Recognise their natural pace and think like a gardener so that when they burst onto the scene, they already have a strong root system. Quick fixes tend to have short lives.

Issue No. 93 – March 2005

Feedback – and forward

Some time ago I had trouble with a professional advisor. It was not so much that his advice was incompetent as that his staff lacked the necessary procedures and his attitude was one of self-protection and justification rather than customer care.

When my complaints created resistance rather than resolution, I told him that "Feedback is a gift". He did not get the message and I would have taken him to court if I had not resolved the situation through another advisor.

Recently, we had an opportunity to prove the point. Someone tried to use our e-commerce system with a foreign currency and I received a frustrated phone call. I could not understand her problem as the system was working perfectly for me as I talked her through it. When we could not resolve the problem I sent her the product by email with our compliments.

In return the lady kindly sent me a screen shot of the problem page, and as a result, our technical team was immediately able to discover a bug in our computer code and put it right.

What could have become a complaint was welcomed as feedback and did us a good turn. Feedback is a gift.

There is another concept, that of feedforward.

I have recently been writing to people who have applied to Brefi Group to become associates. Unfortunately, some of them had not included contact details on their CVs and I have been unable to tell them of the special offer that is available to them. They did not think forward about how their CVs might be used.

I learned this lesson early in my career. I submitted a proposal for a design project to a major institution. Eventually, when I had heard nothing from them for a long time, I contacted them. They were still interested and I did get the contract. But they had been unable to contact me.

I was confused. I had submitted the proposal with a covering letter on company headed stationery with full contact details. However, the proposal had been separated from the letter when it was sent to the decision maker. There was no contact information on the proposal itself.

Lesson learned. Now every Brefi Group proposal has contact details as a footer on every page!

I first came across the concept of feedforward in the book *The Art of Systems Thinking* by Joseph O'Connor and Ian McDermott. I quote from their text:

> "Feedforward describes an interesting and slightly different effect of some types of feedback. It comes from our ability to anticipate the future. It is when the anticipated effect in the future, which has not yet happened, triggers the cause in the present, which would otherwise not have happened. Thus the future reaches backwards to affect the present. For example, when you expect to fail, you often do. After all, what's the point in trying if it's a forlorn hope? When you expect to succeed, on the other hand, your energy and optimism help you and make it more likely that you will. Nothing succeeds like success. (And nothing fails like failure.)"

Issue No. 94 – March 2005

The best advice I ever got

I am a great devotee of *The Economist* magazine. It arrives every Friday and I devour it from cover to cover; it normally takes me a whole week. I start at the back with Books, then Science and Technology, then Finance and Economics, then Business, then though the regions of the world. I am a believer in the freedom of the individual, free trade and the power of the human mind. *The Economist* gets behind the news into explanations and principles; it helps to see the bigger picture and to recognise the trends and forces that are shaping the future.

The other magazine that I read is *Fortune*. This arrives on the same day, but fortnightly. I tend to read it first. It is more of a magazine, with in-depth business articles. The current issue celebrates 75 years of publication and includes two articles of great interest. One is their ultimate reading list of 75 books that teach you everything you really need to know about business.

The other is an article based on asking 28 leaders about the best advice they ever got.

I noticed a theme and a couple of parables. Here are some extracts:

Do what you love

Donny Deutsch (CEO of Deutsch Inc) from his father:

"Look, whatever you do in life, find something you love – I don't care if you are garbage man – and everything else will fall into place. If you love something, you'll be great at it, and the money will come and everything else will fall into place."

Ted Koppel (anchor at ABC's Nightline) from Danny Meenan after he said that he wanted to go into politics:

"You would be a lousy Congressman and it looks like you are going to be a pretty good reporter. You will have much more fun being a reporter than being a Congressman. And you should do what you're good at, and do what you love. And you look to me that you are loving journalism."

Jim Collins (author of *Good to Great*) from Peter Drucker after he said that he wanted to start a consulting firm:

"Drucker asked, 'Why are you driven to do this?' I said I was driven by curiosity and impact. The huge thing he said to me was, 'Do you want to build ideas that last, or do you want to build an organisation to last?' I said I wanted to build ideas to last. He said, 'Then you must not build an organisation.'

"His point was, the moment you have an organisation, you have a beast to feed – this army of people. If ever you start developing ideas to feed the beast rather than having ideas that the beast feeds, your influence will go down, even if your commercial success goes up – because there is a huge difference between teaching an idea and selling an idea."

Parable 1:

Vivek Paul (President and CEO of Wipro Technologies) from an elephant trainer:

"The best advice I ever got was from an elephant trainer in the jungle outside Bangalore. I was doing a hike through the jungle as a tourist. I saw these large elephants tethered to a small stake. I asked him, 'How can you keep such a large elephant tied to such a small stake?' He said, 'When the elephants are small, they try to pull out the stake and they fail. When they grow large, they never try to pull out the stake again.'

"That parable reminds me that we have to go for what we think we're fully capable of, not limit ourselves by what we've been in the past."

Parable 2:

Anne Mulcahy (CEO of Xerox) from a customer:

"When everything gets really complicated and you feel overwhelmed, think about it this way: you gotta do three things. First, get the cow out of the ditch. Second, find out how the cow got into the ditch. Third, make sure you do whatever it takes so the cow doesn't go into the ditch again.

"Now, every time I talk about the turnaround at Xerox, I start with the cow in the ditch. The first thing is survival. The second thing is, figure out what happened. Learn from those lessons and make sure you've got a plan in place to recognise the signs, and never get there again."

Issue No. 95 – March 2005

What is your life for?

I have recently returned from a visit to Saudi Arabia. In the cultural guidebook I read before I left, there is a statement that fascinated me. It was to the effect that Saudi Arabia is a very good place to work if you want to save money. Since there is no public entertainment or anything else to spend your money on you can save a lot of money.

Many people stay for a couple of years, send money to their families and return home. But some stay for ten years just for the sake of saving money. The implication was; deny yourself for ten years and you can become (materially) rich.

It seemed to me that it is rather pointless deliberately to deny your life pleasure for the sole purpose of saving money with which to buy pleasure later. Money is a means to an end, not an end in itself. What is life for? To deny life's pleasures is a form of martyrdom.

Many of us have this weekend been celebrating Easter, in memory of one Middle Eastern Jew who allowed himself to be sacrificed for the benefit of others. We hear a lot these days of modern martyrdoms – often at the cost of other people's lives. But even at the root of these martyrdoms there is a belief in benefit for others; it could be said that true martyrdom, therefore, is an act of love, a gift.

But I know people for whom a milder form of sacrifice, maybe for their families, is more a selfish act of self-justification than a joyous gift. What is life for?

When working with individuals and organisations

Brefi Group consultants often apply Robert Dilts' Neurological Levels model, the highest level of which addresses this issue. In different versions it is described as 'purpose', 'spirituality', 'connection with the outside world'. This is the level at which inspiration and leadership can appear. It matches well with the top of Maslow's hierarchy of needs – self-actualisation. These touch people's personal mission in life.

If an organisation can connect with the higher purposes of its members, then people will be inspired to work with the organisation. Issues of motivation, retention and stress will disappear and the organisation will behave as a high powered team.

What is the purpose of your life? What is the purpose of your organisation? In each case, whatever you find, notice how it is really a means of achieving personal fulfilment.

That is why Brefi Group's slogan is "Releasing Human Potential". Release someone's potential and you help them fulfil their potential – and become more complete human beings.

Issue No. 96 – April 2005

Change what you can

I have been much struck by this week's Letter to the Editor from Rob Smith. I remember a personal development tape that took the same theme. If you must worry, then find somebody on the minimum wage and pay them to sit in a corner and do it for you! Then get on with your life.

I quote a well-known prayer of my mother's:

God grant me the **courage** to change the things I can change;
the **serenity** to accept those I cannot change;
and the **wisdom** to know the difference.

One of the main processes that I use when coaching is setting well-formed outcomes. The first requirement is that the outcome is phrased in the positive.

The second is: "Is the achievement of this outcome within your control?
"What do you need to achieve it?"

This can be really powerful when used during a meeting. How many times does a group spend time discussing things that it cannot affect?

Take note of Rob's advice and spend your life changing what you can.

Dear Editor
The best piece of advice I have ever received is "Do not worry about things you cannot change".

I have always wondered where my father got his laid back view on life from; nothing panics him and he just deals with 'problems' or difficult situations as they occur, rather than worrying about future events that he can't control.

Two years ago we found that he had cancer. The family were devastated and rallied round to support and help him through this terrifying experience. Whilst chatting to him in hospital one day I admitted to him that I was worried that he might die from the illness. He turned to me and said: "Why worry; you cannot influence whether or not that may happen, anymore than I can. If I die you will need to deal with any issues that arise; if I don't, then the worry will have been for nothing. Worrying about anything beforehand serves no purpose."

Since that day I have lived my life by that mantra. I feel more relaxed; I take things in my stride and I don't worry about things. I also give this as advice to friends, family and colleagues, and they agree that it does seem to work. At the end of the day, if you can do something to help the situation then do it. If you can't, then review the situation regularly in case something changes, but until there is something that you can do to improve the outcome, just relax and let things happen.

Regards
Rob Smith
Senior HR Advisor
DAS Legal Expenses Insurance Company Ltd

Issue No. 97 – April 2005

What is safety?

Wherever we go we are surrounded by situations and environments that are potentially dangerous. I am currently working in a very large heavy engineering plant. Forklift trucks drive around, cranes move heavy objects, there is machinery and dangerous materials. Safety is the top priority here.

But how do you measure it? I don't think you can. You can measure accidents – but we try to avoid those. You can record potentially dangerous situations. But how do you measure safety. Indeed, what is safety? Is it just an absence of danger?

We should all be conscious of safety. The home is the most dangerous place to be, with hot saucepans, and carpets and cables to trip over. Similarly on the roads, probably the most dangerous travel is on foot. And in the office there is not only the danger of kettles, filing cabinets and cables, but in many countries a legal responsibility to ensure safety.

So what is safety? It is an attitude of mind, an awareness and a set of processes. You cannot measure safety in the workplace, but you can train people to follow procedures. But you must be vigilant – it is very easy to destroy a good culture in a moment of thoughtlessness.

Many years ago I worked in another major plant with heavy machinery. There was a breakdown, which potentially would have cost the company a lot of money. The engineers managed to get the plant back on line faster than had been expected. The plant manager congratulated them. However, he failed to point out that they had succeeded by taking some risky short cuts. They had got away with it on this occasion, but by apparently condoning such practice he had in fact undermined his own safety policy and increased the likelihood of an accident in the future.

This week's book review explains how attention to small details can achieve major changes at the tipping point. In a factory it is acceptance of an over full litter bin or a greasy floor that can lead to a major disaster. Check on the little things and the big ones will be taken care of.

Issue No. 98 – April 2005

HRD 2005

I thought you would be interested in some of the developments at Brefi Group, so I am making a change to the editorial style this week to report on our highly successful stand at Britain's largest training and development exhibition HRD 2005.

Last year we attended the Confederation of British Industry Showcase in Birmingham. Our objective then was to raise our profile in our target market of corporate bodies. HRD is different; it is the main shop window for training and development and an opportunity for us to meet clients and prospective clients. We had a busy three days.

Although Brefi Group offers a variety of services in consultancy, facilitation, executive coaching and training, we were advised to focus our stand in one area only. We are launching a range of products that address two major concerns in training:

It is increasingly difficult to get managers to release staff for training – and even more difficult for senior professionals to find time for themselves.

However good the training is, something like 80% of it gets forgotten after the course, unless it is rapidly and repeatedly reinforced and applied.

Our solution is "90-MinuteLearning" in which we offer an intensive 90-minute workshop on an organisation's premises, followed by ten multi-media follow-ups over the next four weeks. This means that participants need to spend only as long as a typical meeting away from their desks – and yet get more effective learning than they would retain from a full day workshop with no follow up. This is proving attractive to clients.

Brefi Group training is designed according to accelerated learning principles under the guidance of accelerated training guru Lex McKee, author of *The Accelerated Trainer* and principal of the Registry of Accelerated Trainers.

Lex is co-operating with us to deliver a series of general purpose accelerated learning workshops that will demonstrate the difference between traditional training and accelerated training. These will appeal to anyone who works in the modern world. Subjects include:

- Learning to touch type in two hours.
- Speed reading.
- Time management, goal setting and personal organisation.
- Using visual thinking tools and techniques to think faster.

The World Speed Reading Champion, Anne Jones, is able to read at 2,600 words per minute under the pressure of competition, with 80% comprehension. She uses the same techniques as Lex teaches and we were delighted to welcome Anne on to our stand.

BuddyCoach™ is a free on-line training needs analysis system that enables individuals to develop their own personal development plan. PodcastLearning is a means of delivering audio lessons that can then be listened to either at a desktop computer or at other times an iPod or other MP3 player. Watch this space for announcements as products come on line.

Me? I am off to New Orleans for a holiday!

I shall be back at my keyboard next week, fully re-freshed, but maybe a little jet lagged.

Issue No. 99 – April 2005

If you had to choose a pope?

Well I'm back. A wonderful week of rest and relaxation followed by a night flight with only a couple of hours' sleep and return to 3,000 emails! Not only that, but Outlook could not cope with so many and kept restarting – so that I actually had 9,000! A major job cleaning them off webmail, and then sorting out my Outlook.

And now, back to work. I have been to New Orleans. You can always find something to learn from, and this week I found a wonderful poster entitled "Peter's Laws". I transcribe it below, with a source in case you would like your own copy.

It seemed appropriate to me. New Orleans is built below sea and river level. Why would anyone do that? It is surrounded by levees and protected by powerful pumps. I think that Peter's 20th law must be: If you find a difficult place to build, get on with it.

I love to travel in the USA. I am interested in language and it is a joy to be surrounded by such positive phrases. In the UK the classic response (often after having put right a mistake) is "No trouble". In the USA it is "You're welcome". Such a difference. I asked a man on the hotel reception to record my loyalty card details. What did he say? "It will be my pleasure." Beat that.

This has been a week when a congregation has elected a pope. How would you do that? I have been reading a book by James Surowiekcki called *The Wisdom of Crowds*. He would say that you need to satisfy the conditions of diversity, independence and decentralisation.

When I have finished the book I will review it for you.

Brefi Group has a management exercise, the Spaceship Shortlist, which challenges a group in the same manner as perhaps the cardinals were exercised on Monday. The key is to decide the criteria before debating individual cases. In all my experience of running it, I have never known a group do this. They prefer to get straight down to business.

We have been running *CorporateCoach* as a blog since January. If you link across to the parallel article, you can add your comments. These will be posted after they have been moderated.

Having just returned, I shall be back to New Orleans in a week for the CoachVille Conference. Lots to learn there! I hope to meet more of you there, too.

Peter's Laws: The Creed of the Sociopathic Obsessive Compulsive

1. If anything can go wrong. Fix it! (To hell with Murphy!)
2. When given a choice - take both!
3. Multiple projects lead to multiple successes.
4. Start at the top then work your way up.
5. Do it by the book...but be the author!
6. When forced to compromise, ask for more.
7. If you can't beat them, join them, then beat them.
8. If it's worth doing, it's got to be done right now.
9. If you can't win, change the rules.
10. If you can't change the rules, then ignore them.
11. Perfection is not optional.
12. When faced without a challenge, make one.
13. "No" simply means begin again at one level higher.

14. Don't walk when you can run.
15. Bureaucracy is a challenge to be conquered with a righteous attitude, a tolerance to stupidity, and a bulldozer when necessary.
16. When in doubt: THINK!
17. Patience is a virtue, but persistence to the point of success is a blessing.
18. The squeaky wheel gets replaced.
19. The faster you move, the slower time passes, the longer you live.

Issue No. 100 – May 2005

Time for a change – what is RSS?

This is our 100th issue of *CorporateCoach* – time for a bit of a change.

Since the beginning of January we have been running a blog (web log) in parallel with the *CorporateCoach* newsletter. This has been to test the technology while we have upgraded the website and migrated to a new server.

There are two advantages of a blog:

It is pull technology, rather than push. This means that rather than us sending you an email that your IT system might reject (and which falls among the hundreds of other emails that you might receive), your computer trawls the Web and downloads new articles when they are published.

There is a formal, though moderated, means for you to comment on articles, rather than just through letters to the Editor.

To encourage you to discover the feedback mechanism, we are publishing our first discussion paper in this issue. John Duncan has written a short paper on self-esteem. This is a subject at the core of coaching. Indeed, one of my associates told me the other day that in some research he had been doing, self-confidence and self-esteem came out as the primary need.

I very much look forward to publishing your comments and suggestions, recommended books and techniques.

Monday, probably when you read this, I shall be flying back to New Orleans for the CoachVille conference. I am very much looking forward to this. Four days sitting back listening and learning with some leaders in the field, and the opportunity to renew acquaintances made last year and to make new friends. If you are attending, please make yourself known to me.

In the meantime, here is John's article:

Enhancing and maintaining self-esteem

Self-esteem is a fragile thing, even for successful people. If not grounded in a real evaluation of self-worth, it can be dependent on such ephemeral qualities as job status or material wealth. In this world of constant change these can be so quickly affected by outside forces resulting in a damaging effect on a client's self-esteem. Working on helping clients in this area can sometimes be an integral part of the coaching relationship.

The first, and to me the most fundamental step in building self-esteem, is to open up the client's eyes to the possibility of change and to imbue in them a self-confidence to accept what is in reality quite a daunting challenge – taking responsibility for their own future. This is all about taking control and not drifting aimlessly in a sea of unpredictable currents. This leads to the next step of generating a curiosity about the limit of their capabilities. Coupled with the self-confidence generated earlier, they can then start to push the limits of their comfort zone and to see that with their newfound self-esteem the potential for growth is phenomenal. A third self-esteem booster is to help the client lift their energy levels. When all three are combined we have a formula for action, and without that, then nothing will be achieved.

A word about comfort zones. Comfort zones are like

open prisons. They set the limits of our horizons and constrain our choices on how we lead our lives. If we never break out of them we will never know what our exact potential really is. But comfort zones are just that – comfortable. It takes a degree of courage to move out from them. In her list of five truths about fear, Susan Jeffers (1987) said that:

"The fear will never go away as long as I grow."

I believe that there is a direct correlation between our comfort zones and the level of our self-esteem. If we can encourage a client to set a goal beyond their current level of self-esteem, then their ability to grow is dramatically enhanced, leading ultimately to the realisation of their full potential. But a word of caution: it is imperative that clients have a full range of support systems available to them during this process.

John Duncan was a colleague of mine and a Brefi Group associate. We worked together in the automotive industry and on a major management development project for a large steel works soon after he qualified as a coach. He later joined me on a promotional tour to Dubai and agreed to move out there for three months to establish our Middle East office. Unfortunately, on his return he was diagnosed with lung cancer and died a few months later.

The universal view was that "John Duncan was a gentleman".

CorporateCoach

The chapters in this book were originally published in the weekly e-newsletter *CorporateCoach*.

CorporateCoach is a weekly email newsletter for senior executives and teams in organisations interested in using coaching to improve corporate performance.

Written by Richard Winfield, it has been published since 2001 with an eclectic mix of thought provoking commentaries, inspiring stories, book recommendations and detailed lessons on how to apply a coaching or organisation development aid.

If you have enjoyed reading *Reflections of a Corporate Coach*, then why not subscribe and receive a new article every week.

www.corporatecoach.co.uk

Richard Winfield

Acknowledgements

It will be obvious reading this book that as a committed learner I learn from people, books and events at random.

However, there has also been a formal journey in which some people in particular have played a part. Here is a selection:

Samantha Winfield: As a young civil engineering student I was fortunate to fall in love with someone studying social work. As a result, I was exposed to psychology, human development and live case studies at the kitchen table. Seeking the holy grail of understanding the dynamics of this relationship has been the subliminal motivation for the rest of my life.

Tony Robbins: *Awaken the Giant Within* and, later, "Unleash the Power Within" were my introduction to the formal world of personal development.

John Seymour: John Seymour and Michael Neill laid the foundation for my knowledge of NLP. It was much later that I realised just how wide and thorough this foundation had been.

Sue Knight: Sue Knight, Lorraine Calland and Ian Ross were a magical team that enabled me to integrate what I had learned. They also extended NLP into business and added emotional flesh to an intellectual skeleton.

Robert Dilts: Robert Dilts has been a prolific writer, teacher and developer of NLP. I have some very thick workbooks as evidence of time I have spent with him.

John Grinder and Richard Bandler: These two did the original research and created the concept of NLP. I have studied under both, but learned mainly from their books and their disciples.

Roger Hamilton: Roger Hamilton is the creator of Wealth Dynamics and a proponent of entrepreneurial business. I have studied with him in UK and Bali, and meet up each year to hear his readings of future trends.

T Harv Ecker: Harv Ecker is the master of integrating ideas and teaching them to large audiences, and Blair Singer is his guru. I have travelled the world to benefit from them both, and from the community of Quantum Leapers that they have created.

Andrew Halfacre: Andrew Halfacre has been senior trainer at Brefi Group for many years. He has also been my e-book publishing mentor with this book project.

Chris Walker of Expressive Design, for the covers of my books and the graphics on our web sites.

My thanks to these and many other influences in my life.
    To find out more about Brefi Group's activities consult these web sites:
    www.brefigroup.com
    www.invisible-coaching.com
    www.ASECcoachtraining.com
    www.brefipress.com
And, of course:
    www.RichardWinfield.com

Brefi Group

Vision

Brefi Group believes in a world of work that enables individuals and teams to achieve their potential in a congruent and ethical manner.

Mission statement

"Brefi Group helps individuals and teams in organisations discover and achieve their potential so that they can become more effective with less stress."

Values

Underpinning beliefs: -

- Each and every individual and organisation has the potential to achieve more.

- As individuals and organisations are aligned and discover their potential, corporate performance improves.

- As individuals are aligned and discover their potential, they impact positively on the wider society.

We value: –

- Learning and development. We role model learning and behave as co-learners when working with clients. We are committed to our own personal and professional development.

- The practice and maintenance of high ethical and professional standards.

- The individual's knowledge of their own business and available resources.

- The bottom-line impact of personal and professional development

- The well being and performance of individuals at work, both separately and as members of teams.

www.brefigroup.co.uk